SKINWALKER RANCH
THE UFO FARM

RYAN SKINNER

ALSO BY RYAN T. SKINNER

SKINWALKER RANCH, PATH OF THE SKINWALKER
&
SKINWALKER RANCH: NO TRESPASSING

Currently available on Amazon and Create Space

ISBN: 9798353801955

A Voodoo Creations book
Published by Voodoo Creations LLC

Copyright © 2015 by Ryan T. Skinner

All rights reserved. No part of this book may be reproduced or transmitted in any form whatsoever without prior written permission from the author

Cover by Ryan T. Skinner

CONTENTS

INTRODUCTION 4

THE ENCOUNTERS 5
   FIRST ENCOUNTER 5
   SECOND ENCOUNTER 8
   THIRD ENCOUNTER 11
   FOURTH ENCOUNTER 12
   FIFTH ENCOUNTER 16
   SIXTH ENCOUNTER 19

THE INTERVIEWS 21
   THE PARACAST WITH GENE STEINBERG AND CHRIS O'BRIEN 21
   THE CHURCH OF MOBUS RADIO—THE MIND CEMETERY 28
   LOCAL RADIO STATION (WISCONSIN): DISCOVER JAMESVILLE 32
   JAMESVILLE COMMUNITY RADIO, MILWAUKEE AREA 36
   MOE BANSHEE'S PODCAST, JANUARY 2014 39
   THE PARACAST—THE GOLD STANDARD OF PARANORMAL RADIO, JANUARY 19, 2014 44
   THE PARACAST—THE GOLD STANDARD OF PARANORMAL RADIO, JUNE 29, 2014 52

CONVERSATION WITH LOCAL RESIDENT & RANCH NEIGHBOR 58

CONVERSATION WITH INSIDE INFORMANT 66

RANCH PHOTO ALBUM 70
   RANCH LAYOUT 70
   THE RIDGE 73
   THE GATES 85
   ON THE RANCH PROPERTY 88
   DRAWINGS AND OTHER RENDERINGS 102
   FORMATIONS AND PHENOMENA 115

INTRODUCTION

Prior to writing this book, I had published two previously, each dealing with the subject of Skinwalker Ranch in Utah. Since then, I have participated in multiple media programs—on television, through radio, and online with various Paracasts—sharing my experiences and encounters with the paranormal and UFO community. Here for the first time I have chronicled in print those conversations and narratives, making them available for those who prefer to read and internalize at their own pace.

The first part of the book seeks to detail in narrative form the experiences which I shared in my first book, <u>Skinwalker Ranch, Path of the Skinwalker</u>. However, here I have done so in a much more straight forward manner devoid of my own thoughts, supposition, and philosophical interpretation, providing only the exact details of those encounters.

The second part of the book is a narrative form of each of the interviews and media programs which took place following the publishing of both books. I have made a concerted effort to enhance each of these interviews with new perspective based on what I have learned and experienced since their airing. Also included are two contemporary conversations I had recently with individuals intimate with the Ranch. Both detail information which can be found from no other source.

Finally, the third part of the book provides a generous selection of some of my favorite photos, renderings, and sketches of the Ranch, the surrounding area, structures and places which play a part in my books, and the paranormal entities and creatures encountered by me and others. Each photo is presented with a detailed description, stories of interest, and brief historical reference.

THE ENCOUNTERS

PREFACE

Prior to 2006, I had never heard of Skinwalker Ranch or had occasion to travel within its vicinity. I had no reason, therefore, to expect my life would undergo significant change as a result of my experiences there on I-70, south of Roosevelt, Fort Duchesne, and the greater expanse of the Uintah-Ouray Indian Reservation.

My first book, <u>Skinwalker Ranch, Path of the Skinwalker</u>, grew from my desire to share these specific encounters with those of the paranormal community, and readers in general, and in a way that conveyed the deep psychological and emotional imprint they had on me.

Following publication, however, and despite the relative popularity of the book, I have received a fair degree of criticism as to the writing style—particularly the figurative language and references, and therefore made the decision to present the content of that book in a more straight forward narrative.

Here follows each one of those encounters, starting with the entities which pursued us along that isolated highway, my first visit to the ranch, the spirit which intruded upon my home in Wisconsin, and ultimately my face-to-face meeting with the Skinwalker itself. I have also included, for the first time anywhere, an isolated encounter which took place at a later date, and which may or may not have been a UFO.

FIRST ENCOUNTER

I had my first encounter with Skinwalker Ranch and the associated anomalies in 2006 while driving with my significant other from Wisconsin to Las Vegas. We are in my car on I-70 south of the Uintah-Ouray reservation in Utah. I have been driving the whole time and decide I am in need of a break. We pull along the side of the road and my companion—my wife-to-be—takes over behind the wheel.

We have been back on the road only for a short while when she says there is a red light behind us at quite some distance but moving up quickly. I look back through the rear window and see it too. However, it defies logical explanation. It is too high up to be an emergency vehicle, such as a policeman or ambulance, and too low and too small to be an airplane or helicopter. At the time, though, it remains little more than a curiosity, and we go back to the task at hand, which is getting to our hotel in Green River.

Within moments my companion is again concerned with the presence of this light anomaly. It is not only in clear view, but has gained on us considerably. However, before I can position myself to get a really good look at it, it again disappears.

Somewhat curious, but not yet alarmed, we resume our travel, driving along a few more miles before the inside of the car is suddenly brightly lit by the sudden reappearance of whatever it is that has been following us. I have my companion pull the car over and I get out. Even to this day I'm not sure why.

Once outside the car, almost irrationally, I examine it for any sign that the source of light is the car itself. It is then that I notice I am bathed in a glow. Turning around, I find myself confronting this ball of light, almost like a red-flamed fire—a road flare suspended in mid-air, hovering only feet from me and about eye-level. For a brief period of time after it is as if my will is not my own, that this intelligence—this thing—has taken over my mind and body so it, in turn, can get a look at me.

The next thing I remember, my companion is shrieking. By this time she, too, has gotten out of the car. Her cries draw my attention to three other balls of light out in front of the car, still at a distance, and approaching. Near panic, I instruct her to run around to the passenger side and I jump in the driver's seat and we speed away.

From there we come across a roadside rest area. These lights still pursuing us, we pull in with the hope that the presence of others will scare it off. Sure enough, the lights by-pass us and disappear up and over a ridge. The rest stop, however, though populated with multiple vehicles—mostly trucks, is completely deserted. I flash my headlights, beep the horn, and yell out some, but there's no response. Not a single person shows himself. The whole thing goes beyond explanation.

With no other choice, and seeing no further sign of whatever was following us, we take back to the road in proximity to Thompson Springs, only a half hour or so from Green River. We have been back on the road only minutes when we start passing isolated cars parked off the shoulder of the road, all with doors or windows opened, but no one in sight.

After we passed the first two, which are fairly close to each other, I have Iryna, my fiancé, slow the car as we approach the next one. I try to get a look for any signs of distress. But other than the look of having been left behind—and keep in mind we're in the middle of the desert with nothing around, there's nothing. Finally, as we come across yet another, and this all within a mile or so, I have her pull over and I get out and investigate. There upon the back seat of the car are some items which clearly belong to a child and an article or two of clothing. But again, no sign of any person or where they may have gone to.

With no other recourse, we get back on the road—I'm driving, intent to get to Green River as quickly as possible. Only minutes later, my companion sees the light anomaly again coming towards us, this time from back in the desert out off to the side of the road.

My first instinct is to get out of there at top speed. Iryna, however, chides me for my timidity, and throws up in my face the number of times I have wished for just such an encounter, and now that I have one, I don't have the nerve to play it out. So I make the decision not to flee, but instead to use the camera I have in the bag in the back seat to capture this thing on video. I then put the car in reverse and drive backwards, the wrong way, on the highway.

However, when I get back to the spot where I believe this thing to be, there's nothing there. Disappointed, I put the car back in drive. Only moments later, my companion again warns me that these light anomalies have returned. I tell her to start recording with the video camera, but she's scared and complaining that with the window open it's too cold.

The situation then develops that there are three of these anomalies, each coming at us from a different direction. I make the decision to stop the car and basically confront them. At the moment, it seems like the thing to do. However, we do remain safely within the vehicle.

As has been the routine up to this point, all three of the anomalies again disappear. Within seconds however, they're back again, all three there in formation and glowing red. I have my companion roll down her window so I can get a better look; they are on her side of the car.

Right before our very eyes, these three balls of light suddenly start to materialize into alien-like beings, very similar to those depictions often seen in movies and media reports: anthropomorphic, thin-limbed, and with large almond-shaped eyes—you know the ones. They, too, look to me to be wearing some sort of wetsuit-like garb with elongated tubes coiled around from one side to the other.

As shaken as I am, I attempt to communicate with them, but receive little more than a curious expression in return, and this by only the tallest of the three there in the middle. The other two, given my position in the car, I can't see as well. Regardless, they are just standing there, neither appearing hostile nor making any attempt to get at us.

At this point, I make for the camera which my companion has replaced in the bag on the back seat, point it at the passenger side window and press record. The battery light initially shines green and then immediately blinks to red. The battery is dead. This I am thinking at the time is not possible. I had fully charged it before we left and had used it only for a couple of seconds since then.

With no other option, and still afraid to a degree of what these alien-like beings may do, I decide not to try to drive away, but instead tell my companion to roll up her window. But she is non-responsive. I notice then that she's frozen, as if with fear or in shock. Her mouth is agape and her eyes wide. I reach across her and roll it up myself.

I'm not sure how long we sit there, the windows all fogged up by condensation, but as the sun begins to come up, the aliens seem to dissolve into thin air and are gone. I turn the key in the ignition. The vehicle starts right up. And we leave.

To make short of the rest of this part of the experience, we have no more encounters with strange phenomena the remainder of our trip.

SECOND ENCOUNTER

After my fiancé and I return from our trip, and with my curiosity piqued, I do some investigating on my own as to UFO and unexplained encounters in that part of Utah. It was then that I uncover the story of the Sherman family and their ranch, which, coincidentally enough, is only about 60 miles north of the highway where I encounter the light anomalies and the alien beings. I decide this is as good a place to start as any. Although there is more to the story in terms of developing a greater familiarity, I ultimately reach out to another individual who has significant experience in and around the ranch and we make arrangements to meet in person. I fly out to Utah. He meets me at the airport in Vernal. I rent a car, and I follow him out to an area in proximity to the ranch, which I believe at this time, may be the source of my encounter.

With this individual joining me in my investigation, our intent is to access a specific part of the property. However, it is well-known that the ranch is patrolled routinely by armed security—all ex-military or police—and that trespassing is discouraged. Trespassers are not treated kindly.

Anyway, it is dark by the time we pass through Fort Duchesne and reach the point in the road where we have to turn into the desert. My fellow investigator is immediately concerned about security and we proceed basically without our headlights off road and in the direction of a nearby creek. Once we reach the creek, we are obligated to drive across it and move deeper into the stark landscape in order to reach the point where the ranch is accessible by foot. The crossing is minimally adventurous, but without serious incident we reach the place we are looking for. We set up a basic camp site consisting of a fire pit and a couple of lawn chairs. The plan is to sleep in our individual vehicles.

Shortly after 9:00 pm, we start off on foot towards the ranch property. It is called both Skinwalker Ranch and UFO Farm. We have only been out in the desert for a brief period, walking up a ridge line, when we hear clear, sharp voices—tense and authoritative. It sounds as if orders are being barked through a bullhorn, but not in any language I have ever heard. My first thought is that it is the local police, the Ute police, speaking in some Native American language. We even see red and blue lights lower down the ridge and flashing from behind some hills, much in the way official lights would look. I am convinced at this point that we have been detected and we will be arrested.

Unsure of what our next move should be, we crouch down and take cover beside a rock formation and wait for the inevitable. The voices go on for a matter of minutes, and then just like that, both the sound and the lights are gone. Curious, I leave my place of concealment, make my way over to the hill beyond which the light was coming, climb up and over to the other side, and find absolutely no sign of anyone having been there. I had expected to see, at the very least, tire tracks. I learn later on that disembodied voices are one of the more common anomalies associated with the ranch surroundings. I have no clear explanation that provides for the lights.

That particular experience behind us, we then move further up the ridge where we come across tall towers from which are strung the high-tension wires providing power to the area. While these are mundane enough, as we get beneath them, they start to glow and hum in a way I have never seen or heard before. The noise is near-deafening, like an approaching train, and electrical charges are clearly visible as they run in steaks of bright white and bluish-white along the wires, every now and then arcing from one wire to the next. It is as if some power is trying to keep us from going any further. Ultimately, we decide that is as far as we will go that night and instead return to our campsite.

The weirdness out there, however, is not quite done with us. We are sitting outside our vehicles, a small fire upon the ground, smoking cigarettes and talking when I notice these small blues lights, as if embers from the fire or some kind of liquid electricity, but instead of sparking up into the air and then descending to the desert floor, it seems as if they are originating there upon the ground and then climbing on their own up into the night sky. So animated are they that I thought they might be fireflies. But instead they are like little balls of energy. I try to record them with my camera, but for some reason they don't show up. Nevertheless, they become a common sight at night while we are out there; as if unconcerned with our presence, they simply go about their business.

That next night, we again try to access the property. This time we make it all the way up the ridge and to the fence line around the ranch. Despite the No Trespassing sign, I pass through the barbed-wire and onto the property. My partner refuses to follow. He assures me, though, that he will maintain contact via walkie-talkie.

Alone, I make my way deeper onto the property and beneath the heights of the electrical towers, which within seconds start their infernal chatter and disturbing light show. Continuing on toward the ridge, I become aware of this pale glow which appears just beyond a hill there before me. It begins as little more than a halo barely cresting the rise. But then it materializes in form much in the way of those that we encountered out on the highway, though distinctively different. As if it has a will and mind of its own, it starts directly towards me. I am immediately overcome with a sense of dread and the impression that it intends me harm.

Nevertheless, I stand my ground, access my camera, and prepare to capture this entity on video. However, just as I prepare to record, I feel as if I myself have been blasted in turn, a flood of dread and fear like I have never felt before coming over me. I lose all sense of time and place. At this point, all I can think to do is turn and run—even if thinking is not the right word. It is more a clear message which materializes in my head on its own. That message is move now or die.

I run down the slope of the ridge and back towards the fence, feeling the whole time that this thing is in pursuit. My instincts taking over, I extinguish the infra-red light that I am using to light my steps, and in the pitch-dark of the night, dive beneath some low branched trees and brush at the base of these car-size rocks. I lay there barely breathing for fear I'll give myself away. However, whatever it is, I have given it the slip or it has on its own departed.

Eventually, my isolation is interrupted by the voice of my companion coming over the walkie-talkie. Shortly thereafter, I am back in camp, no worse for the wear, other than the destruction of some of my equipment in which I have invested no few dollars.

THIRD ENCOUNTER

After returning to Wisconsin, I start having these weird, unexplainable, and routine intrusions. It starts with late night knocks on the door, which of course when I go to answer, have no origin. At first I think its kids in the neighborhood knocking and running. But logic tells me it's too late at night for kids. Besides, there aren't that many kids where I live, and given the size of my property, as big and as open as it is, there's no place to run to.

These episodes then elevate to an unmistakable presence in my house, and always late at night as I make my way to bed. The cat, however, seems to be quite aware of these intrusions, often acting spooked or hissing when there's nothing there to be seen. Many nights consecutively I find myself waking to the sense that someone is in the room with me, that something is standing over me, or that I am being watched.

These paranormal events go on for a matter of months, until after one particularly disturbing episode in which this entity, perhaps considering making its presence known in some way more substantial, stations itself outside my bedroom door, squeaking the floor boards as it shifts its weight from foot to foot. Having had enough, I yell out to it that its nonsense is no longer an issue for me, it can continue if it likes, but I will no longer pay it any heed. Shortly after that, all indications of its presence cease and I am again alone. My wife, having lost patience with my growing occupation with the paranormal and its seeming interest in me, has by this time taken our child and moved out.

FOURTH ENCOUNTER

Following the paranormal encounter with the entity there at my house in Wisconsin, I convince my brother to take a trip with me out to Utah. I feel the need to go back to the ranch, as if drawn there by some power over which I have no control.

Once there, we rent a vehicle and make the drive out into the desert north of the ranch, and pretty much to the same spot as my trip with the other researcher. This time we are equipped with a small tent, some sophisticated night vision technology, and high end cameras—on which I spent quite a bit of money. We also have a liter of vodka.

Unfortunately, that first night, my brother drinks a little bit too much, well into a state of inebriation, and is probably not in the best shape when we set out that next day to do some exploring of the surrounding desert. He winds up twisting his ankle navigating the uneven terrain. As a result, he is unable to come along with me as I head out that night to approach the ranch. He, instead, crawls up inside the small pup tent we have. I leave him with one of the walkie-talkies, the range of which is serviceable, and we come up with some protocol for communicating, in case someone or something is listening.

Talking back and forth with my brother most of the way, he complaining about his sore ankle, as well as his stomach and a headache, I hike across the open desert, up the ridge, find my way through the barbed wire, and make for the spot which overlooks the ranch property. Prior to passing through the rocks, I let my brother know we'll probably be out of range for a while, and I suggest he gets some sleep. He agrees, but assures me he'll leave the walkie-talkie on as a precaution.

By the time I get myself settled down it is getting dark. All I can see without the aid of the night vision glasses is the indistinct forms of some cattle down in the fields and the soft glow of the lights to the house and the security trailer.

As I nestle there between the rocks, confident that I am out of sight of any potentially spying eyes—ranch security, I use my night vision glasses to scan across the property. First, I fix upon the bait pen in field one for a while, but it's empty. I then look out towards the trees to the south and west, but there's no activity. There's also nothing of interest back towards the house and trailer. Overall, it is really quiet and I'm not seeing or feeling anything out of the ordinary.

Just when I'm feeling disappointed and thinking I'd head back towards my brother, I suddenly hear this thumping noise coming at me from the direction of the ranch and echoing off the rock surrounding me. I can't help but notice it is coming nearer. Now straight up over my head, it takes on the sound of helicopter blades. However, I see nothing that would suggest there is a helicopter anywhere above my position—no lights, no nothing. I notice, too, that the cattle below me within the pasture are showing no reaction to the noise.

Convinced that I've stumbled upon some advanced military technology—or it upon me, I sit down on the rock, light up a cigarette, and wave vaguely to a pilot I can't see, but I'm sure is looking down upon me. I'm sure he's communicating with the ranch and it's only moments before security descends upon my hiding spot and I'm handed over to the local authorities. But instead, the sound clearly starts moving off, heading out into the desert. As it does, I notice it sounds less like the muted chop of helicopter blades and more like the slow, ponderous flapping of a pair of gigantic wings. Regardless, I sit and finish my cigarette. No one is coming for me.

No sooner do I grind the orange embers of the butt into the stone, the walkie-talkie comes alive and it is my brother. He is very intense. Barely able to control himself, he tells me that all kinds of weird stuff is happening all around him.

First he tells me that after we broke off contact, he dozes off. He then starts having these really intense dreams, so vivid he thinks they are real. He tells me the details. Then, he hears a car engine, loud—as if it is right outside the tent, and whoever it is, he is revving the thing as if he wants him to know he's there. He says he wants to get up and check it out, but he finds he has no control over his body, as if he is paralyzed. Then as suddenly, it is gone. Shortly thereafter his limbs and extremities again start to respond and he is able to move.

Intent on taking a look around, he grabs his flashlight and exits the tent. Almost immediately, the brush and low-topped trees around him start to come alive, rustling as if with thousands of birds. Suddenly, the space above the brush fills as the birds, all at once, lift from the branches. As they rise, they form into this one massive triangular shape, as if becoming a singular body with extensive wings. Higher into the darkness it lifts and then begins to fly off. It is then that he raises his flashlight to shine upon its form, and just as immediately, and as if by a huge spot light, the kind that needs to be mounted, his entire surroundings are lit up. It too, however, lasts but a second and everything again goes dark.

As we are talking, then and there, his voice fills with the closest thing from him that I ever heard nearing fear, and he tells me the thing with wings is descending upon him. Everything then goes silent; he's taken his finger from the walkie-talkie.

With no option but to wait it out, I sit there. Only minutes later, he is back, his voice really excited, and not in a good way. He tells me whatever it is flying around, it is now gone. It takes me a moment or two to get a word in, but I tell him it's cool, that all this stuff is normal out here. I tell him I'm a good two miles or so away, and that I'm heading back.

No sooner do I get these words out, I hear coming from the rocks up over my head the sound of voices, very similar to those that I heard that first time I was here. The tone is commanding, in a language with which I am unfamiliar—it sounds like a cross between Native American and something eastern bloc, amplified but localized—meaning it is not echoing or bouncing off the rock, and as if coming down out of the sky. I hush my brother and tell him I can't talk, I'll get back to him as soon as I can. I then turn the volume down on the walkie-talkie almost as low it can go.

There in the dark, I have no idea who or what is up there, whether in the rocks or hovering in air, and all I can think to do is crouch low, press up against the rock, make myself as small as possible, and await that one chance to make a run for it. Then seconds later, the voices are gone, and all I hear is the silence of the desert canyon. That's when I hear the walkie-talkie burp, and then my brother's voice. I can barely hear, but it sounds like he says, "It's got me." I turn up the volume, but all I hear is static and what seems to me to be garbled speech, but as if removed or distant. Afraid that he is in some sort of trouble—my first thought is the reservation police, I gather up my gear, make my way through the narrow pass, and start jogging back towards camp. But even at a steady stride, it's about two miles and twenty minutes or so.

Despite the heavy boots and the equipment, I keep up the pace without too much effort—the night is cool and there's only the slightest of breezes. Probably within fifteen minutes, I recognize the lay of the land: the campsite is just ahead. As I get to the top of the rise, the SUV comes into sight, the light from the moon reflecting from a variety of surfaces. As I start down, and only a few hundred yards away, the walkie-talkie springs alive. My brother's voice comes over comparatively strong and clear. He says there is something there with him, something trying to get at him. Again, the walkie-talkie falls silent

Running as fast as I can, I cover the last bit of distance to the tent, my brother nowhere in sight. Passing the vehicle, I throw myself into a slide right up to the front of the tent. Finding the zipper to the flap, I tear it down and fling the flap aside. There sitting in a pure state of panic is my brother, staring off into the nothingness and the bottle of vodka held upside down by the neck and raised like a weapon. But other than that, he is alone. There is nothing there.

Keeping back beyond arm's length, wary of the way he is holding that bottle, I say his name and let him know that I'm there. I have to repeat myself a number of times, but I manage to bring him back to the present before he cracks me over the head. For the next few minutes, I assure him he's okay, that there's nothing here, nothing trying to get at him. I tell him he was probably sleeping, and it was all sort of a nightmare. But he's not buying it, convinced it was real. He tells me that he was sure he was being attacked by something and all he knew was that he was ready to fight for his life.

After that, we stayed up most of the night, sharing with each other what it was we experienced over the last couple of hours and making sure the contents of that bottle were put to good use. In the morning, both of us with a bit of a hangover, we pack up and leave.

Since that trip, I have been back to the surrounding area multiple times, and as a result have built wonderful relations with no few neighbors who have been generous in sharing with me not only their own experiences with the ranch and the other entities for which the area is known, but also stories and encounters they have heard from others. As for me, I have experienced many different wonders myself and will continue to go back to the area until I have satisfied all the questions that remain.

FIFTH ENCOUNTER

I have a flight to catch back to Wisconsin after spending an extended period of time camping out in the desert surrounding the ranch. I am delayed by a number of minor issues and arrive at the airport too late and miss my departure. As I can't arrange another flight until later the next day, I decide to catch up with one of my fellow investigators who is still out there and go out to the ranch one more time. As soon we meet up, we waste no time driving out to the point that provides access to the ridge overlooking the property. Skipping the part about getting myself settled in, come twilight we make our way along the ridge intent on getting to a site which brings us as close to the ranch property as possible and which offers a direct line of sight overlooking the fields.

Significantly more familiar with the lay of the land than the previous trip here, and with significantly enhanced gear and equipment, the fellow researcher and I head out towards Werewolf Ridge. We make good time up the landscape, pass the barbed-wire fence and no trespassing sign, along the ridge, along a length of rock slab that looks like a bunch of dominoes lain side by side, as if it is the remnant of some ancient road, pass among dozens of different rock formations of various size and shape, and eventually reach the top of the mesa leading to Werewolf Ridge. Aware that we are clearly visible to ranch security in the open flat land that lies before us, we take off jogging towards the ridge, intent on getting under cover as quickly as possible. We expect ranch security to appear at any time.

As soon as we reach the ridge, we pass between these rocks towering on both sides and come out in a spot overlooking a white construction-type trailer and a dirt road leading to a gate upon which is hung another no trespassing sign. A little further away there is a second trailer, also white in color, and the ranch house, which is nothing special—no different than the others I have seen on the surrounding properties. We also see, not too far off, one of the bait pens. Within this same perimeter, there are three wood poles upon each of which is mounted surveillance cameras and lights. Knowing that if we stay out in the open we can be spied from below, we move back into the shadow of the rocks and setup our camera equipment. We then settle in to wait patiently for any potential activity.

I'm not sure how long we are there, maybe a couple of hours. All I know is I am getting tired and, admittedly, a little bored. Then as we are contemplating calling it a night, I notice a single yellow orb, no greater than the size of a softball, moving among the grazing cattle, who seem to take no notice. I point it out to my companion, and he notices it too. Then we see another one, and then another, until there are eight or nine of them, maybe more. Wasting no time, we both grab up our cameras and begin shooting video and taking photos.

At some point, I put down my camera and pick up night vision optics. I train the glasses upon where the orbs are grouped together there below me. Suddenly, three of them move away from the group and make for the ranch house. While two climb up over the roof, the third heads for the pole upon which the lights and camera are positioned. The house lights up in a pale glow, and then a shower of sparks cascades down from the top of the pole. The house and trailer both go dark.

Moments later, the door to the trailer opens and one of the security guards exits, cursing and heading towards the post. Once there, he accesses a transformer box and seconds later the lights come back on. Oddly enough, I notice that he is being trailed by one of the orbs of light every step of the way, but he never stops to take notice. My imagination perhaps getting the best of me, I have a momentary thought the two are somehow connected, perhaps even working together; or, at the very least, that it is some sort of technology for which at the time I have no rationale. My point is that there is no way I could conceive of that the guard can't see or doesn't know the orbs are there. Since that day, however, and given what I have learned, I am convinced that the guard was at that moment fully unaware of the presence of the orb.

Regardless, the power restored, the guard goes back inside the trailer and closes the door. The orb of light then poises there as if contemplating what to do next. As if decided, it turns and joins up with the others which have come back down from the roof of the ranch house. Together they move back towards the cattle and slip among the dozens of others which have since materialized out of the darkness. I turn for an instant to glance over at the other researcher and he is looking back at me. We're both shaking our heads as if we can't believe what we are seeing. As we turn back to the scene below, there in the middle of the field, we watch as three of the balls of light—could be the same ones, I guess—separate themselves and move straight in the direction of where we are concealed up on the ridge.

As they move towards us, we lose sight of them, the ridge falling away at an angle that creates a blind spot there below our position. They are out of sight for what seems like five minutes, during which the two of us both exchange the field glasses for the cameras. Then without warning, they silently rise up just above our position, not much more than an arm's length away and as if looking down upon us. We find we are immediately lit up by these beams of orange-yellow light which these orbs are pointing down upon us. I am as scared as I have ever been in my life, and from the reaction of my companion, he is feeling something similar.

Together we take cover behind the rocks. As we do, these balls of light settle to the ground just beyond where we are—no more than ten, maybe fifteen feet, bathing the stone all around us in this greenish-yellow glow. I am doing the best I can to get my camera in an angle to record what's happening while at the same time keeping as little of me exposed as possible. I'm too focused on what's going on to see what my companion is up to.

As I'm watching—and not through the camera lens—this black swirling mist materializes as if out of nowhere. It is dark and somewhat translucent, even gelatinous, with only enough mass to give it the look of something substantial. As I'm staring into this murky dark against dark, much like a shadow, it begins to take form. Then, as if it steps out of nothingness or through some unseen portal, there standing before us on all fours, no more than three to five feet away, is the wolf. It is massive in size, with thick, black matted hair, a large bushy tail, also matted and dirty. It stands there looking at us, its eyes dark and flat. It shows no aggression and no fear. I'm guessing it stands there for about three minutes. All the while, I am thinking should I run, approach and attempt to pet it, or maybe try to scare it away. But I'm frozen in place. Then it just turns, walks into the darkness, and disappears.

Once it is gone, it is as if we are released from a spell. But before we can orient ourselves, or even exchange some words, we hear what sounds to us like the voices of the guards. They are coming over walkie-talkies and quickly approaching our location. Aware that to be caught here is more trouble than it is worth, we quickly gather up our equipment, scramble through the rocks, and set out to escape over the mesa and back to the cover of the desert.

It isn't until we get back to our campsite that we have the opportunity to check our cameras to review the video we managed to record. Even though we both admit that we were too distracted or scared to directly video the appearance and presence of the wolf, we are both certain that we had the cameras running at the time and expected to have not only something from the encounter, but also everything that we had videoed leading up until then. However, when we play back the recordings there is nothing. It was as if everything had been erased, as if the very time line never existed.

SIXTH ENCOUNTER

I am out in the desert with a group of other researchers not too far from the ranch. Since most of the activity, especially the orbs of light, occurs at night, we are all seated around the fire pit nursing a few adult beverages, talking among ourselves, and looking out into the landscape for signs of any anomalies. With nothing to report and the late evening turning into early morning, everyone else decides to call it a night and get some sleep. I am left to myself, sitting comfortably in my lawn chair, my video equipment at my side, and looking up over the ridge and into the star-filled sky.

As I'm watching—it's about 4:30 in the morning, marveling at how much different the sky looks out here as compared to Wisconsin, I get this premonition, almost like a voice in my head. It tells me to put aside my camera and video equipment and it will reveal itself to me. I know, it sounds crazy. At the time, I'm thinking so too. I look around, but there's no one there. I'm by myself. However, as I have experienced quite a few things out here that defy explanation, I do what the voice asks. I gather up my gear and bring it over to my car, open the door, and put it inside.

Having complied, I return to my lawn chair and sit. Only seconds later, there over the rise, appears this football-shaped object, about the size of a car, and bathed in an orange aura. It is definitely substantial and quite real. It then begins to move in my direction, seemingly with caution, but steadily.

Unable to resist the need, I jump up from my chair and run over to my car, set on getting to my camera and getting photos of the object. As I see it, it is my one chance for proof that there are UFOs out here. I get all the way back to my car, get the door open, and even get my hand on the camera; all the while the object continues to move towards me. However, as soon as I bring the camera up and manage to point it in the direction of the UFO, as if it is watching the whole time, it immediately speeds off and is gone. I never get the chance to snap the shot.

THE INTERVIEWS

The PARACAST with Gene Steinberg and Chris O'Brien

On September 2, 2012, I had the opportunity to do an interview following the release of my first book, The Path of the Skinwalker. The interview took place on the Paracast with Chris O'Brien and Gene Steinberg. David Weatherly, another ranch researcher, was also part of the show, as was a Ranch security guard who for the purpose of anonymity is referred to as Chip. Here for the first time in print is a snap shot of the content of that interview.

As most readers are already aware, the Ranch came to the attention of the paranormal and UFO community after the Sherman family shared their story with Zach Van Eyck, a reporter from the Deseret News in Vernal, Utah, and after selling the ranch property to Robert Bigelow, in 1996. The Sherman's story was then turned into a book written by George Knapp and Colm Kelleher, called Hunt for the Skinwalker: Science Confronts the Unexplained at a Remote Ranch in Utah. While the book has been relatively widely read, and is accounted by some as a significant resource on the ranch and paranormal phenomena in general, it also, in parts, lends itself to questions as to credibility.

CHRIS O'BRIEN, CO-HOST

Chris O'Brien, one of the hosts, claims to be among the earliest journalists or researchers to uncover the phenomena regarding the property. He reports that the Shermans, who bought the ranch in 1994, claim to have experienced a variety of different paranormal anomalies or events while living on the property, including over-sized wolves and other strange creatures, disembodied voices filling the air over their heads, strange crafts exiting portals or apertures on the ranch, and a connection between digging on the property—wells, for example—and an increase in these types of incidents.

O'Brien then goes on to make the statement that he is responsible for the sale of the ranch by the Shermans to Robert Bigelow. Having become aware of the story through Van Eyck, O'Brien relates that he took the drive out to the ranch and met with Terry Sherman, a man whom he found to be both sincere and honest, even downplaying some of the events which were perhaps embellished in the telling. He then mentions wanting to sell the ranch, concerned for the safety of his family, but that he also wouldn't want anyone to go through what he was going through. O'Brien says that he suggests both Lawrence Rockefeller and Bigelow, and just happened to have the phone numbers of both on hand. Sherman then, supposedly, called Rockefeller, but couldn't get through to him. Coincidentally enough, Bigelow reached out to him shortly thereafter, and the deal for the sale was made.

O'Brien then goes on to claim that he was on the phone with Sherman during the infamous incident with the three dogs. He says as he was in conversation with Terry Sherman, the blue orbs appeared, circled about the house, and then were pursued by his three ranch dogs off into the trees. At this time, Sherman says to him that he has to call him back, his dogs just ran off. Those dogs were then found the next day reduced to grease piles. O'Brien said this happened in August of 1996, not April of 1995, which was the date indexed in the book by Knapp and Kelleher.

O'Brien then goes on to acknowledge the role of NIDS and BAASS, inferring that for the last 16 years (at the time of the interview) scientific research and observation has been taking place there at the Ranch. However, he also admits that no hard data relative to identifying any specific phenomena, or proof that anything out of the ordinary, in that time, has been made public by NIDS or BAASS. Second-person reports, to this point, are the primary resource. He does cite law enforcement involvement in a number of cases, without getting into what they are.

DAVID WEATHERLY, RESEARCHER

David Weatherly, a recognized paranormal investigator, has spent significant time while living in Utah following up on incidents in Fort Duchesne, Vernal, and Roosevelt, among other areas of the state. He's considered an expert on the ranch and the Uintah Basin in particular, but also on the subject of paranormal events in general, and throughout all of the Four Corner states. He makes the point that this type of activity takes place throughout the basin, and not only in proximity to the ranch.

In particular, he refers to a park north of Vernal which lies within the Ashville National Forest called Dry Fork Canyon. He mentions, specifically, the suicide of two individual males, who six months apart, climb up to a cliff, disrobe, and leap off. Bigfoot or other Sasquatch-like creatures have also been seen in this area, as well as humanoid-like beings similar to grey aliens or to the Little People popular in European mythology. According to Weatherly, sightings of these Little People are relatively common in the basin, particularly up in the mountains or caves. They are known to play music and dance and are considered mischievous. One story he relates is of a group of campers who stumble upon a group of these Little People dancing deep in the canyons, and when they are noticed, prior to disappearing practically before the very eyes of the campers, they present as annoyed with the intrusion.

Weatherly goes on to acknowledge, however, that physical evidence of these Little People, or any other entity, is limited to undistinguished footprints and vague photos. Of these, the most common is of a bipedal or anthropomorphic wolf-like dog-man, the likes of which has been spotted leaping from roof top to roof top in Roosevelt. The Ute Native Americans living in the area have many stories of similar sightings.

Chris O'Brien then introduces me as a late-comer to the research on the Ranch, in as much as I have not been, prior to this time, as richly involved as he and Weatherly. O'Brien acknowledges the time I have spent in the vicinity of the ranch, and an experience he and I had together while we were out on the ridge. He gives me credit for investigating and documenting the phenomena at the ranch and for having experienced it directly.

With regard to tales of the Little People, one of the visitors to my forum, a Native Ute, tells a story of when he was a child in which he was playing outside and encounters a group of these Little People. They were dancing around. They spoke to him in a language he did not understand. He went over to join them, but then his father came upon the scene and pulled him away. The Little People vanished. I was to discover later, and this was verified by Weatherly, that Native lore tells tales of the Little People luring away unattended children, after which they are neither seen nor heard from again. In addition, the Native people believe that the Little People dwell beneath the ground, and that these termite-like mounds which are fairly common out in the desert and in the canyon are actually chimneys from which, according to eyewitnesses, smoke can at times be seen rising.

CHIPS, RANCH SECURITY PERSONNEL

Chip, not his real name, is a ranch employee known to me. He was one of the guards hired to provide security at the ranch, a job that he kept for about 8 weeks on and off, working shifts of two weeks at a time. He describes the ranch as a strange place, and the local people, primarily Native Americans, as extremely superstitious and influenced by folk lore.

According to Chip, he is not much of a believer in the paranormal, and other than the ranch being in a place that is rather isolated, he says nothing out of the ordinary was happening out there—not at first, at least. Later when he returned for subsequent stints, he would notice that his possessions would get moved around without explanation. For example, he would have an item in a specific place, his bag, perhaps, and then when he would go to get it, it wouldn't be there. This was happening all the time, without explanation. He even recalls a stereo—portable—which, although unplugged and without batteries, turned on by itself.

Chip goes on to say that he no longer works there at the ranch. In fact, none of the people with whom he worked are still involved with the property. Nevertheless, he suggests most of the guards were residents of Las Vegas, Nevada. To get to the ranch, they were flown into the airport at Vernal; he infers it was at the expense of BAASS. However, that routine was soon to change. The officials at BAASS came to believe that the TSA agents at the airport, having learned to identify the security personnel due to their gun permits and weapons, were providing independent paranormal and UFO investigators and researchers with the details of their arrival and departure. In this way, these investigators and researchers were free to attempt to access the property with minimal concern for being detected or detained. As a result, the security teams were required to drive rental cars from Las Vegas to the ranch, which was an approximately eight hour trip.

As for their guns, according to Chip, they were required to be armed, or so he was told, to deter trespassers. They were directed to patrol at night and keep people off the property. Most potential trespassers, however, were local teens and problematic only during the weekends. They would drive up to the gate or gather to drink beer somewhere just off the property. It was more nuisance and nonsense than anything serious. Security would simply scare them off, or if they weren't causing any trouble, leave them alone. Rarely, he said, were serious investigators a problem.

Chip, however, believes the guns were for some other reason; primarily, that there was something out there from which they needed protection. To support his contention, he explains that they were also equipped with cameras, night vision glasses, and thermal detectors. They were also directed to pay heed to any emotional or physical changes they themselves experienced, for example a sudden and unexplained chill, hairs standing up on the back of their neck, and other events of this sort. They were to then stop whatever they were doing at that time, and immediately start to snap photos of their immediate surroundings and scan with the glasses and thermal detector. The only explanation for this behavior they were provided was that there was an unexplained energy associated with the ranch.

    Chip acknowledges that the only objects he detected on the photos they took were orbs. These orbs were, according to what he was told, balls of energy. He, however, says that he did some research of his own on light anomalies and orbs in photos, and believed them to be dust and pollen. He concluded otherwise, after taking 25 photos consecutively. Some would have hundreds of orbs and the very next one, snapped literally less than a second later, would have none. He then goes on to explain—contrary to the claims of others—that there was no correlation between the incidence of these orbs in terms of frequency of appearance or quantity and an increase in the paranormal activity on the ranch, saying that he experienced nothing else out of the ordinary. He does add that he at times felt weird, especially when alone in the dark and cold, but attributes such feelings to the extreme isolation of the ranch and his own mind playing tricks on him. He says he can think of no correlation, in his own experiences, between the orbs and any other unexplained incident or paranormal encounter.

    As for the dogs on the ranch, which many other individuals refer to as guard dogs, or trained dogs, or go so far as to infer some degree of elevated aggression, Chips insists they were no more than regular, everyday household pets. They had no specific training of any sort, for example the type received by police dogs. He does believe, though, that this was strategic, in as much as BAASS officials preferred an animal that would, ostensibly, provide a natural reaction to any paranormal encounter. He does recall a number of occasions on which, for no explainable reason, a dog would become submissive, lie down on the ground and roll over on its back.

    With regard to outside belief that there was an extensive and sophisticated video monitoring system in place throughout the ranch, Chip revealed that the camera boxes affixed to the elevated poles around the vicinity of the ranch house and in the fields were, in truth, dummies. They contained no actual video equipment or even the wiring required to make them operational. In fact, the cameras one time housed in those boxes were during his time there sitting in a closet within the security trailer, and had been long before he arrived.

Asked about the presence of scientists or other formal investigators, Chip says they were there only one time during his shifts at the ranch. Their activity, however, amounted to very little, and he saw no formal experiments or significant effort with regard to observations or study. It was his opinion that they were merely indulging the whim of Mr. Bigelow, and at the same time collecting a pay check. He also confirms the rumors that there were some high-ranking military personnel who showed up at the ranch, but it was before his time. In addition, he acknowledges that security personnel was required to submit urine samples at any time they claimed to have seen or felt anything associated with the paranormal—apparently to rule out any sensory issues, such as being under the influence of some substance, such as alcohol or marijuana. These samples, however, sat around until the guard returned to Las Vegas, and then the urine was tested. Brain scans were also done on some of the guards, but the guards were not permitted to see the results.

While I raised the possibility that suspected encounters perhaps might leave physiological evidence within the brain of the person who has the encounter, Chip stated that he was unaware of what BAASS might be looking for, other than something out of the normal. He suggests the military was directing these tests, but he has no explanation. He believes they may have had some sort of new military technology they were developing out there and that the security guards were really just lab rats. The purpose of the MRI was to see the effects, if any, of this new military technology. This is all supposition by Chip, however, and speculative at the best.

Sometime in late 2009 or early 2010, Chip was let go from his security position at the Ranch, as well as was everyone else with whom he had been working. In addition, from what he understood, another 50-60 employees associated with investigating the ranch but housed in Las Vegas were also laid-off at that time. He attributes the decrease in staff to the loss of funding which was being received from the NSA. He states he can verify he was being paid through that arrangement, inferring that the checks he received indicate as much. Chris O'Brien confirms he has seen reliable and verifiable documentation to support Chip's claims.

OTHER NOTES OF INTEREST

Chip says that he did hear the story of the dog-man. He mentions BAASS officials were sent from Las Vegas to investigate the sighting. He knows only that photos were taken of the footprints left behind, as was a plaster mold. A similar sighting was also investigated down in New Mexico.

As for trespassers at the gate, I was informed by a trusted source that the gate had at one time been pulled from its foundation by attaching it to a chain to the back of a vehicle. No sooner had the gate been pulled free, a helicopter—small and black—reportedly came up from behind a hill and pursued his car to the highway. The fact that a helicopter would have had to be sitting prepared and ready to do so would suggest something more nefarious or secretive was going on at the ranch. That gate has since been replaced by concrete barriers.

Chris O'Brien suggests that the fear emanating from the individual generates the manifestation of the Skinwalker and the other unexplained entities that are encountered in the vicinity of the ranch. I, in turn, suggested there may be a military variable and that the emotion of fear is generated by some sort of military technology being developed there on the ranch.

In addition, I reference a recent snow storm during which local residents in and around Roosevelt report seeing a mother ship, a UFO, and at which time all electrical power is knocked out. The local power authority, however, attributed the loss in power to a blown transformer, further explaining that the light anomaly others believed to be from the UFO was actually the arcing of that transformer.

THE CHURCH OF MOBUS RADIO—the Mind Cemetery

During this interview with Chip, the host, I spoke initially of that first encounter I had while traveling with my fiancé on I-70 in Utah, focusing primarily on my inability in the moment to come to terms with the fact that I was actually experiencing the paranormal. After all, I had been told me whole life that these things don't exist. Yet here was this substantial entity—definitely not human—only yards away from me. It was an encounter which ultimately spurred me on to become an active researcher of the paranormal, and the Ranch in particular.

This narrative then led me to share what I had heard about the Meyers. They were the family that lived in the house prior to the Shermans. While there in the home, they experienced the intrusion of seemingly intelligent golf ball-sized orbs of light. These orbs not only zoomed and hovered about the property, but actually made their way into the house. So disturbing were these intrusions that the family would secure themselves inside a central family room for safety, and were required to bolt and secure all the cabinet doors and kitchen draws to keep them from opening and closing on their own.

THE NATIVE AMERICANS

In my many conversations with the local Ute—though they do not speak freely on the subject, I have come to understand that they accept the presence of these paranormal entities as co-inhabitants of the lands upon which they live. There is no doubt, as far as they are concerned, that these entities are real, that there are alternate dimensions or planes which exist alongside the one in which we live, and that there are those who can travel freely from one to the other. Their general approach is to leave them undisturbed, to avoid the areas in which their presence is strong, and if encountered, to let them go on their way.

I share their opinion that whatever is out there is spiritual, not aliens or visitors from other planets. These entities are, for a lack of better words, angels or demons moving from a parallel dimension that exists here alongside of us, traveling back and forth through a portal or portals linking the two. The Ranch property, so it seems, happens to be the location of one or more of these portals; there are others in the surrounding canyons. Personally, I don't believe there is any government conspiracy or advanced technology associated with the Ranch, and that if advanced science or the government is involved, it is because they recognize there really is something going on out here that is supernatural or paranormal and they have a desire to learn what may be behind it all.

BIGELOW

I myself have never had any direct conversation with Bigelow, but have been contacted by his attorneys. This contact has to do with my physical proximity to the property, alleged contact I may or may not have had with Ranch personnel, information that I have disclosed on my website, and comments I may have shared with regard to others associated with the Ranch, their activities, and some of the more grandiose claims they have made.

One of the concerns I did share, however, was the influence which Bigelow's associates, primarily through BAASS, managed to exert over the efforts of the Mutual UFO Network, and like organizations, to investigate potential UFO sightings and then share those findings with the paranormal and UFO community. When BAASS contracted with MUFON to share information, the result was the creation of extensive secrecy and a sort of black hole out of which information no longer flowed.

FIRE FIGHT WITH ALIENS

There was an overseas conference in Europe. One of the participants mentioned that there was a fire fight on the ranch between aliens and Ranch security in which one or more researchers were killed, and as a result NIDS, the predecessor of BAASS, and its officers made the decision to disassociate itself from the Ranch. Of course, there was no physical evidence that such an incident actually took place. Since then, there have been statements floating about that Bigelow, convinced that there is nothing of interest taking place on the property, was in the market to sell it off. However, in the past he has made other statements with the seeming intent to mislead the curious, such as insisting there is nothing scientific or technological taking place on the property, and that security is no longer present.

Nevertheless, there is some truth to the fact that the paranormal activity in and around the Ranch has diminished over the last few years. That said, there are locals that insist that activity levels seem to rise every ten years or so. Two of the more recent, according to other investigators and eyewitnesses, were balls of light exiting from a number of different caves in and around the ridge along the Ranch, and the sighting of the opening of a portal from which a large, black figure crawled out of and then loped off into the desert. There is also the report of a bipedal creature peeking into the windows of some of the homes in Fort Duchesne. Allegedly, the local police pursued it down a neighborhood road but lost it in the darkness.

THE WOLF
I have never seen or encountered while investigating the Ranch a wolf or any canine-like creature standing up on its hind legs or having any appearance I would consider humanoid. I am also of the opinion that the Knapp and Kelleher book exaggerate the size of the wolf, as does the movie, which suggests it as big as a small car. In fact, the entity I encountered, which although every bit wolf-like in appearance, was only somewhat larger than average, and definitely nowhere near to being compared in size to a car.

Further, while other investigators, such as Haas Lohrs when upon an Apache reservation, claim to have shot at a Skinwalker, or a wolf-like creature thought to be a Skinwalker, I go out into the field without a firearm. First, I do not want to give Ranch security a reason to use their weapons were we to have a chance encounter, or officers from the Bureau of Land Management, for that matter. Second, I have yet to encounter any life form out in the desert, natural or paranormal, which requires the need to consider deadly force. Even the wolf entity I encountered presented as docile, showed no indications of any aggression, and walked off having shown little interest in our presence.

As for sightings in an around the ranch, one source is a tricky stretch of road in Randlett, south of Fort Duchesne, which is referred to as Dead Man's curve. According to the locals, there's a wolf which will run alongside passing cars. Every now and then there'd be a collision which would damage the car, sometimes significantly, but the wolf, seemingly unharmed, would just run off into the landscape. Supposedly there are plenty of police reports to document these incidents, but no one has been able to track down the offending beast.

RAY (PSEUDONYM)
While the interview was on-going, I referenced a friend of mine, Ray, not his real name—we met due to our mutual interest in the Ranch, who I then

suggested would be interested in joining the conversation. I immediately sent him the call in number. He, at the time of the interview, had been investigating the ranch for more than two years, mostly on the weekends and on a weekly basis.

While discussing the topic of Ranch security, Ray states that each time he approached the property, he was convinced that the guards were ever aware of his presence. He tells, too, of his distant encounters with the ranch dogs, which he refers to as guard dogs. He recalls a particular incident in which at least one of the dogs was barking ferociously and as if attacking. He, however, does not have a line of sight and cannot see what, if anything, is going on. Then there is a sudden yelp, after which at least one of the dogs flee. It is his understanding that the dogs on the ranch would get killed or disappear routinely, and that security went through a lot of dogs.

As that may be, information to the contrary strongly suggests the dogs on the Ranch were not actually guard dogs, or trained dogs of any sort, and that most of their trouble came from unfortunate encounters with porcupines, the needles of which sink deep into flesh, are difficult to extract, and are very painful.

As for one particular experience Ray and I did share, we were out with a group of other researchers, and not all that close to the Ranch. We were up on a rise, looking down into a valley. The other four members of our group already had headed off in that direction. But as we were looking we saw instead what looked to be a group of six, only indistinct and as if shrouded in a sort of aura, a whitish colored light. Unsure, we called down to them, but there was no reaction and no answer. Then, as if they had stepped behind a curtain, they were gone. Encounters of this sort are fairly common out there in the canyon desert.

Ray also had an encounter with a Sasquatch. He and another investigator were out in a densely wooded area. It was dark. They heard something knocking upon the tree trunks. So they set up a flashlight pointed towards the area where the sound was coming from and hid to see if it would attract anything. Only moments later, something was up at their back and growling, and from the sound it wasn't a bear, coyote, or wolf. They froze for a number of seconds out of fear and then took off running.

LOCAL RADIO STATION (Wisconsin): Discover Jamesville

This interview takes place on local programing called Discover Jamesville. For this particular episode, I am the final guest of the show. The host, Yuri Rashkin, and I meet at a local luncheonette. He comes at me from the perspective of a lack of verifiable evidence of my encounters.

Rashkin starts the conversation by asking me how I define myself, to which I answer I prefer the term phenomenalist. It is a term I haven't coined, but which I believe is the best to describe the endeavor. I go on to explain to him that in order to have an open mind on the topic, we have to be able to step out of our preconceived notions of what reality may or may not be. I explain that I believe there is an ultra-reality which coexists along with ours, and that it is more spiritual than alien.

My take on it is that a majority of ghosts and things that go bump in the night, anything that manifests physically, are more related to the demonic, meaning entities that are separate from what we have come to accept as spirits of those deceased. The dead, as we generally accept the concept to be, do not communicate physically. Theirs is more the realm of dreams.

These entities—demons—that manifest physically, either in body or perceptibly through sensory means, fall within the category of fallen angels. In the mythology of yore, they are gnomes and faeries. Today they are the bug-eyed greys (aliens). It is simply a more contemporary interpretation of the same phenomena. I have researched all religion, including Native American, and it all comes down to the same belief—a war in the heavens between two factions of angels. It is these entities which to this day are haunting the earth. As a result of being cast out of the heavens, they exist without physical bodies of their own and that is what they are after. These demons seek to possess humans, taking advantage of any weakness in the individual which leaves them open and vulnerable. It is, I believe, a type of possession, although I do not pretend to be able to explain the mechanism by which it actually occurs.

At this point in the interview, Rashkin inquires about the Ranch and my interest in it. I explain to him that despite its appearance, and contrary to a comment of his, it is unlike any other property in the Uintah Basin. No other ranch, as far as I know, maintains a 24-hour security force, each member of which is ex-military and armed. I then share with him conversations I have had with insiders—those who have formal positions there on the ranch—who tell me of encounters with animals that are not alive, not in the sense that we acknowledge; for example, they leave no thermal trace. Yet they are observed to be fully animated, as if taken over by some paranormal or supernatural force, and may have some connection with the orbs of light which are routinely observed, mobile and seemingly intelligent.

Further, I share with him that there is a government presence associated with the Ranch, and though not as extensive as Area 51, it is suggestive that there is some sort of secretive activity going on there, perhaps with military application. Further adding to the speculation is that the area tests for measurably higher concentrations of geomagnetic activity than any other part of the state and poorer air quality—despite being located a considerable distance from any major city.

Further, and though somewhat of a tangent, I add that the Native Americans, in a more spiritual way, believe there is a thinness in this particular part of the canyons and basin to the force or curtain, whatever you want to call it, that separates this alternate dimension from the one in which we exist, and it is this thinness which accounts for the paranormal activity and the frequency of unexplained encounters.

THE ENCOUNTER

The night of my encounter with the wolf, we, another local researcher and I, come in at night, as we have done multiple times before. As is the routine, we use only night vision gear as to avoid detection by ranch security. It is a three mile hike to reach the destination overlooking the ranch.

Shortly after our arrival, we note the activity of these balls of light down in the field in proximity to the ranch house and guard trailer. We begin videoing. We are certain the video we are capturing is going to create a buzz throughout the paranormal community. It is crystal clear and we are getting plenty of it.

As for the balls of light, they have shape and dimension. They are bright and pulsating, and every now and then, would power down and disappear, almost as if someone flicked a switch. Nevertheless, using high-end video equipment, we are certain we are capturing the activity.

Then without warning, the power suddenly goes out in the security trailer below, and all the windows go dark. We watch as no more than a quarter of a mile from our spot, the guards spill out of their trailer, walking out into and around the property trying to figure out the cause of the blackout. Each guard is being followed by one of these balls of light. The two of us are convinced it is some sort of government experiment—the balls of light and the guards working together. But then it becomes obvious to us that the guards have no idea these balls of light are even there. They rectify the power outage and return to their trailer.

As we continue to watch, the balls of light disappear and reappear. Then three of them break off from the rest out there in the open field and begin to float towards us. I admit the thought of a personal encounter worries me. But then these three also power-off and disappear. They leave no thermal trace. My partner and I, nevertheless, continue to look for them through the night vision glasses we have.

Suddenly, all three appear at once but ten feet above our heads. They are shooting a bright light down upon the two of us. My initial concern is that the bright light will alert the guards to our position and they will be coming for us. However, I abandon that concern as the three spheres come to land less than 15 feet away from where we are standing, their light casting our shadows tall upon the stone at our backs.

Now, it is one thing to read about aliens and the paranormal in books, it is a real game changer, however, to be face to face with the unknown. I am as frightened as I have ever been, and drained of all courage. My mind begins racing, and all I can think to do is try to hide myself behind this two foot rock. Fearing abduction, or something worse, neither I nor my partner are still videotaping.

Finally, I muster the nerve and peek over the rock. I see before me this black swirling mist, almost as if it has mass—like smoke with a solid structure. It is dark against the dark. Slowly, the mist coalesces into a wolf. Not the shape or form of a wolf, but an actual wolf. It is sitting not more than three to five feet away from me. I do not perceive it either as aggressive or friendly. It is staring us in the eye for what seems like five minutes. I have no doubt, it, as do the balls of light, feed off of fear and depression; they create it and feed off of it. Then as casually as can be, the wolf turns around and vanishes into the rocks.

I am not sure of all the details immediately after it disappears. What I do remember is my partner and I running through the desert, having fled after hearing the chatter of the guards coming over their walkie-talkies and heading our way. But we are giddy more than scared, certain that we have invaluable video which will prove the existence of the paranormal. Unfortunately, when we have the opportunity to check the video, it is all gone, as if it never occurred, as if it never happened. It was as if neither one of us had pushed the record button. Two separate cameras, both high-end and properly equipped for the purpose, and both had been compromised by the Skinwalker. To me the absence of the footing remains as some of the most compelling evidence of the Skinwalker's supernatural ability.

JAMESVILLE COMMUNITY RADIO, Milwaukee area

INTERVIEW OVERVIEW

This interview is with the host of a local radio station and is specifically about the book. To start the show, the host asks me what it is I hope to gain from my research in this area. I respond by acknowledging that I have been told by others in the field that the quest for the paranormal is a never-ending journey for which there is no answer. However, I believe what separates me from other UFO nuts is I am tenacious, and as such I will uncover enough puzzle pieces to eventually reveal the bigger picture.

The first of those pieces was found while driving with my wife-to-be, Iryna, along that lonely stretch of highway through Utah. It was then that we encountered that ball of light following the car. No bigger than a baseball, it had the appearance of a child's sparkler, burning red in color and emitting sparks. At first merely curious, we pulled to the shoulder of the highway and exited the car to investigate. It was there hovering but a few feet off the ground and not too far from the rear of the car. Though it made no move towards us or presented in any way threatening, I nonetheless felt irrational fear. I directed Iryna to get back into the car and we sped off. Undeterred by our speed, which was definitely beyond that of the local limit, the ball of light stayed with us. We came upon a rest area, and with the hope of shaking it off our tail, we pulled in and I began honking the horn, hoping to arouse the attention of anyone who would respond. Despite the fact that we were surrounded by cars and trucks, not a single person did; there wasn't the hint of a dome light or headlights. Nevertheless, the sphere veers off into the distant mountains and disappears. It was then that Iryna tells me to get it together, reminding me this is what I've been looking for my whole life. Ultimately, we get back on the highway and again encounter this entity, only this time more intimately. It is this strange episode and what follows which initiates my near-obsession with the paranormal.

THE RANCH

Through my research, I learned about the Ranch—only 30 miles to the north of where I had that first encounter—and its paranormal history, which goes back to at least the early 70s. It was also about this time that I heard strong rumors of military conspiracy theories and a confirmed connection with the NSA. Some of the first locals with whom I spoke told me about the Meyers, the family that lived in the ranch house before the property was sold to the Shermans. They spoke of golf ball sized lights that would appear at night and not only zoom around the outside of the house, but find their way inside also. Allegedly, the family would take refuge in a central room within the house, huddled together against the intruders. It was so bad that all the kitchen drawers and inside doors had to be locked and bolted to keep them from opening on their own.

But the ranch isn't just light anomalies and UFO sightings; it covers all the bases when it comes to the paranormal and supernatural. There have been claims of Bigfoot sightings, poltergeist, a werewolf, ghosts, and other unusual cryptids and phenomena. Here the host comments that this extensive association detracts from any serious credibility, questioning whether any one place could realistically be the source of so many different anomalies. However, my take on it is that the Ranch and surrounding basin is truly a center of paranormal energy, and it is the individual who has the encounter that is perceiving the manifestation of that energy according to his own fears. In other words, it is a form of susceptibility upon which that paranormal energy plays. In fact, according to lore, the Skinwalker is actually referred to as the trickster; it has the ability to toy with the minds of those it encounters, and as such maintains it elusiveness by remaining just out of reach. The host acknowledges the plausibility of suggestion. I then remind him of the possible role of the military to create a form of technology that affects the mind: You see what you fear the most.

In my case, my first encounter as a researcher was the red, white, and blue lights, with the bullhorn barking orders. My greatest fear, at that time, was running afoul of the local authorities, and particularly the reservation police. So that is how the paranormal manifested itself to me. For the three minutes or so that those lights remained flashing and the voices shouting, I was fully convinced the police were there just over that hill and coming for us. However, when it stopped and I had calmed enough to go have a look for myself, it was just me and the lonely desert. The officers' footprints and the tire tracks I was certain were going to be there were nowhere in sight. I am convinced it was the trickster—the Skinwalker—seeing into my mind and playing on my fears. I offer as a further example my encounter with the wolf. Those balls of light and the black roiling mist might have coalesced into some other form were the encounter to have been with some other individuals than my partner and me. We both saw what it was we had expected to see given what we knew.

MY ENCOUNTERS

In response to a follow up question by the host as to how many encounters I have had out there, I chose to avoid providing a number, having had a relatively negative experience with Joe Rogan. However, I did say that I enjoy going out there with those who are skeptical, and then have the opportunity to watch their reactions and expressions when they witness for themselves. The host one again expresses the opinion that my brain is playing tricks on me, which I choose not to deny. However, my position remains that it is not the minds of those who encounter the Skinwalker that are at issue, but the ability of the Skinwalker to manipulate those minds.

MY THEORY

When asked as to my theory, I believe some of it may be tied to the government and portal science. There are those that believe that Bigelow is working on technology that will allow him to transport his payloads, specifically his space stations, into orbit more cheaply. The inference being that either he has a desire to exploit the presence of these portals or discover the physics governing them. He does, after all, have a team of doctoral scientists out at the Ranch doing research and studies.

While I'm not sure how much of this theory applies, I do believe Bigelow and BAASS are trying to glean something from the unique physics at work there on that property. More so, what we consider to be aliens or demons may be a significant part of what is going on there. These portals are gates which open onto some alternate dimension or spiritual world, and out of which move demonic entities with whom we co-exist. It is these entities that we are encountering in and around the property.

Ultimately, I hope my book allows me to share with others what I myself have experienced and provides some insight into this other spiritual or demonic plane.

MOE BANSHEE'S PODCAST, January 2014

THE PATH OF THE SKINWALKER

    This interview starts out with Moe, the host of the show, sharing with me—and her audience—a summary of what she has learned about the ranch. Apparently she has done her research. I add to her knowledge that the Ranch lies within the acknowledged path of the Skinwalker, a stretch of the canyons which is taboo to the local Native Americans. She counters by telling me that it is also within 700 miles of Roswell, New Mexico, inferring a possible paranormal or extraterrestrial connection along some sort of prescribed line. Referring to the ex-military and commando-like guards employed to secure the property, who may or may not be armed with the automatic weapons the hosts suggests, I agree there may be something to her observation.

    In response to her curiosity as to how I started along my path of paranormal discovery, I tell her about my experience out on I-70 with the red glowing sphere. I assure her that despite my personal experiences with the paranormal I had no great interest in UFOs at the time. However, being face to face with three alien entities—as both my girlfriend and I were, and these similar to the stereotypical greys most describe, has a way of changing one's perspective. I'm not afraid to admit it both scared me to death and intrigued me at the same time. After we returned to Wisconsin, I began to read everything I could find about that stretch of Utah and the phenomena associated with it, and that's when I discovered the Ranch. Not too much later I took my first trip out there.

    Since then—about six years now, I have been researching the place. As a result I have become to many the guy with the answers. Contrary to what the host suggests, drawing a parallel with the Ranch and the movie Close Encounters, I don't believe there is an organized effort to drive people away from the area so that Bigelow can go about his activity in secret and without interference. While it is a good conspiracy theory, these types of activities and strange phenomena have been going on well before he bought the property. I do not, however, completely discount the possibility that some sort of military operation has been going on in that area, if not upon the Ranch itself, since the 60s.

    Most of the land in and around the Ranch is part of the Uintah-Ouray Reservation. As a reservation it is as near to a sovereign state as you can get in the United States, and as such has its own laws and law enforcement bodies. I myself have tried numerous times to gain permission from the reservation council to visit different locations with the aim of furthering my research, but have been denied each time, and without reason. While it is possible it may just be that the areas that interest me the most are sacred to the Ute, I am also willing to believe there may be secret activity going on out there, perhaps in concert with the government, which they don't want anyone else to discover.

At this point in our conversation, the host moves away from conspiracy and the extraterrestrial and expresses an interest in the Native American lore associated with shape-shifting. I share with her my understanding that there are different interpretations of what a Skinwalker is, depending upon one's perspective. The original concept as it applies to the history of the Navajo, for example, differs considerably from the contemporary application.

Historically, the Skinwalker was, for the most part, a witch doctor, a medicine man gone over to the dark side. Spiritually speaking, it is the Christian equivalent of making a deal with the devil, consummated by the killing of a relative and the drinking of his or her blood. Through this rather gruesome ritual, the medicine man surrenders his humanity and in the process gains the ability to shapeshift—take on the form of an animal with whom he feels a connection, and most commonly a wolf, coyote, bear, eagle, or even serpent.

These days, however—and although I don't get into too deeply on the show, the Skinwalker, with relation to the Ranch, is perceived as a more spiritual entity which moves between dimensions; or, relative to the Native Americans who live in the Four Corners, akin to the bogey man, inhabiting the back lands of the local reservations and bedeviling folks almost at random.

WHY ME?

My obsession with the paranormal impels me to go where the monster lives, and that means the ranch and the surrounding desert. Despite the fact that I live in Wisconsin and it takes me the better part of two days to drive to Utah, it is a trip I take with some frequency and whenever my responsibilities allow. I have a specially equipped RV which I drive out to a location as close to the ranch as possible, find a spot out of sight, and make myself at home, spending anywhere from a few weeks to a month or more. While there, I spend the hours of the day and night walking for miles to see what I come across. It takes patience and an open mind: these paranormal events and encounters do not appear on command.

As for what I've actually seen, the most common anomaly is the presence of the spheres or balls of light. They tend to present in one of three colors, red, blue, and yellow-white, and range in size from that of a baseball to that of a basketball. While they are clearly intelligent, in as much as they seem to move about with a purpose, it is rare to have any interaction with them. When that interaction occurs, it amounts to being followed—they are pursuing me. However, any attempt on my part to approach them results in their departure. Other than that, the most common is hearing the disembodied voices. They speak in what sounds to me to be English or some Native dialect, but the actual words, while somehow familiar, are something I can never quite make out. Each time the conversation occurs right overhead, lasts 20 seconds and stops.

As for an encounter other than light anomalies and voices, I share a story about a group, a team of investigators, of which I was part. Whenever I'm out there, especially with other researchers, I like to stay up into the night as long as possible, since this is when most of the activity seems to take place. This particular night, everyone else calls it quits around 3:00 am. But I choose to stay up. It is about 4:30 in the morning. I'm sitting in a folding chair and gazing at the night sky, my camera in hand and ready. Suddenly, I get this premonition. You can think of it as a voice in my head. The voice tells me if I put the video equipment out of reach, they will then reveal themselves to me. I leave my chair and go and put my camera in my vehicle. I then return to my chair and sit. As I'm watching the sky, there over the ridge appears this football shaped light. It is orange in color and about the size of a car. It is slowly, but steadily, moving straight for my position. Unable to contain myself, I run back to my vehicle to get my camera. There's no way I'm going to let this thing get away without capturing some video. Camera in hand, I turn back towards my chair and in direction of the approaching anomaly. However, before I can manage to point the lens, it stops, speeds off, and disappears. I have no doubt it was watching me all the way, and once it saw the camera, made a conscious effort not to be videoed.

While to some this incident may seem incredible, there is documentation of a NIDS' scientist who reported receiving telepathic messages of sort from one of the spheres or balls of light. The message was something along the line that these entities were both aware of and watching the scientist, and they were being warned not to interfere. While it wasn't made clear what it was they might be interfering with, the scientist who experienced this contact was adamant that this message was consciously framed in his mind, and stated that he felt as if he was at the time possessed.

THE HOLY GRAIL

The Holy Grail out there is not the Skinwalker, but portals which open up. To the Natives, and perhaps to the government and its scientists, the Ranch is a unique place in the world where the separation between dimensions is least restrictive—think of it as thinning of the veil or curtain separating the two—which allows these entities to move easily back and forth. The Shermans themselves tell of an incident in which they observed what appeared to be an aperture or tear in the night's blackness out from which exited a number of these balls of light.

Why the government is interested in the Ranch has not been to date established. The most accepted theory is that the intent is to take advantage of the singularity of the phenomena associated with the area to advance aerospace or military technology, whether in terms of physical weapons or something psychological. The host, forwarding a theory of her own, suggests the government may be doing some work beneath the surface of the earth, in anticipation of, for example, a meteor strike or some other calamity directed downward from space.

Of course, there is the persistent conspiracy theory associated with the Bottle Hollow reservoir, a man-made lake constructed in 1970, and which is the primary source of freshwater for the area. According to some, there is a subterranean military base of sorts that was built beneath its depths at the time of construction. Witnesses in the area recall an incident in which a UFO was pursued by military aircraft, swooped down low, and then seemed to disappear beneath the surface of the reservoir without resurfacing. A search of the lake's depths by curious investigators revealed no evidence of a craft of any sort or any type of wreckage.

While I myself have never seen a stereotypical UFO out there, I have seen what many refer to as the RV or Chupa. It is a UFO with one headlight out front and two headlights to the back, yet with no physical structure between.

In essence, the body is invisible. This object has been spotted with great frequency, and by many others than me.

CONCLUSION

While my curiosity has grown to a personal obsession, I prefer, when possible, to make my trips out to the ranch with at least one other person. The first reason is because there is an element of danger, and not only with regard to the paranormal. The desert can be an unforgiving environment filled with very real risks. There are wild animals, extreme terrain and weather, and the possibility of getting lost or injured. The second reason is having someone along to validate any encounters. The reason why I continue to focus on the Ranch is because of the frequency of incidents. Finally, regardless of my encounters, or anything I may do to document their veracity, I am thoroughly convinced that there will always be those who will remain skeptical and seek to cast doubt. For this reason, my primary motivation is to prove to myself the existence of this paranormal dimension, and along the way, fulfill my own sense of purpose. I had a lot of paranormal things that happened to me when I was a child, and these are the answers I am looking for. Perhaps, along the way, I will allay the anxiety I associate with death, the fear that what we have in life is all there is, that our existence is a random one. Maybe those answers will be found out there on the ranch.

THE PARACAST—the Gold Standard of Paranormal Radio, January 19, 2014
With
Gene Steinberg and Chris O'Brien

This interview was based on the first book, <u>Path of the Skinwalker</u>. When asked why that title, I explain that it is in part derived from the Navajo belief that the Skinwalker of legend traveled along a particular path, and it just happens that the ranch is located on that path. In addition, there not too far from the ranch and leading out to Werewolf Ridge is a stone formation which has the appearance of a path or highway. It consists of long, rectangular blocks lying side by side and as if placed for a purpose, as if by the ancient peoples. I have always been intrigued by this formation and wonder of its connection to the early history of the land and the original people who may have traveled there long before the arrival of the white man.

As for the term Skinwalker, Gene Steinberg, the host, and an individual with whom I have visited the location, states it is unfortunate that it has become associated with the Ranch, as the lore is not directly associated with the Ute. While accurate in a sense, this claim is not exactly true. It is true that the origin of the Skinwalker lies with the Navajo, but that there is a relation to the Ute cannot be discounted. According to the history of the two people, the Ute established an alliance with the Spanish, and then later with US troops, and worked to drive the Navajo from Utah. In response, or so at least legend has it, the Navajo called upon the dark spirit of the Skinwalker to take revenge upon the Ute. There are those that believe the path of the Skinwalker coincides with that of the Long Walk which the Navajo took south into Arizona while fleeing the harassment of both the white soldiers and their Ute allies.

Later in the interview, Steinberg acknowledges that I have spent more time researching the Ranch and the local phenomena than anyone outside of the scientists associated with NIDS and BAASS, and that my book is the first to relate specific first-person paranormal encounters and experiences there in the surrounding area.

MY FIRST RESEARCH TRIP

I made my first research trip out to the Ranch in 2007-2008. I went with another researcher with whom I have since had a falling out. At that time, the location of the Ranch was generally unknown. Finding it was for us a bit of a scavenger hunt. We actually wound up at a number of ranches before finding the correct one.

Paranormal activity in the area during this period and up until the end of 2009 was notably high. It has since quieted, which according to the locals is not unusual. Periods of high activity are normally followed by less active periods, and the time between the two can stretch as long as ten years. Since that first trip, I have been to the location no less than twenty times, and most recently we—other researchers and I—have located a hot spot removed from the Ranch, but still upon the path of the Skinwalker.

During these trips, I generally spend a week or two deep in the desert in proximity to the Ranch, but not on its property. While there, it is always my goal to encounter these entities, and if possible to interact with them. To date, I have had multiple interactions that go beyond filming balls of light, even if they fall short of actual communication. Beyond those I have shared previously, I have heard two males voices engaged in conversation and as if taking place over my head. The voices are muffled and hard to hear, and appear to be speaking a language somewhat similar to English, but the words of which I cannot quite make out. The voices linger only shortly and then cease. Unfortunately, this has never occurred while I have been out there with anyone else. Nonetheless, it is a fairly common phenomena and has been experienced and reported by other investigators and locals. No one can say, however, with any conviction if these voices are actually aloud, meaning if the opportunity was there to record them, would the recording produce anything, or if it is just a matter of 'hearing things'.

Regarding my encounter with the wolf, I acknowledge that I had prior to read the book by Knapp and Kelleher, and while I may have been influenced to some degree by their description of the wolf, the one I encountered was significantly different. For one, there was nothing supernatural as to its appearance. Though at the time my close-up encounters with wolves in general had been limited, my estimate is though large for a wolf, it wasn't gigantic by any stretch of the imagination, nor did it have an obnoxious smell or the smell of death. In fact, I recall no particular smell or odor of any sort. If there was something out of the ordinary to its appearance, it was that it was dirty and its fur matted, and that it had a tail that seemed bushier and longer than typical.

MY PERSPECTIVE

It is my position that some of the research taking place out at the ranch is being done by government agencies—contracted through Bigelow, and specifically those which are associated with the military. I believe they have discovered some form of technology which will benefit the military. That technology is directly related to the concept of portals, and may have something to do with travel. It is no secret that Bigelow Aerospace has been developing inflatable space stations. To date, these stations have been placed into orbit with the assistance of the Russians, and at no little expense. The theory is Bigelow Aerospace is working to exploit these portals as a means to facilitate the launch of his space stations, and without the cost and limitations of fuels. To substantiate this theory, it is well-known that the FAA has made arrangements to forward any UFO reports directly to BAASS. While such reports or sightings may not have anything specific to do with portals or inter-dimensional travel, it does suggest that both the FAA and Bigelow Aerospace acknowledge the existence of UFOs and that Bigelow Aerospace, at least, expects to glean something of use from this information.

CHIP REVISITED

Chip, the one-time security guard, and I still communicate from time to time. He no longer works for the Ranch, nor in security of any kind, and has since moved out of state. I assume, by this time, his identity is known by Bigelow, and his need for anonymity as it relates to the 'public eye', therefore, is no longer as intense. BAASS simply has no choice but to accept that the proverbial cat is out of the bag. On the other hand, Chip has never been considered a bigtime insider. The information he revealed was not all that fantastic, or in any way damaging.

How Chip and I met is an interesting story. While he was working at the Ranch in 2009, he was directed to make contact with me for the purpose of gathering intelligence, specifically when I would be in the state and around the ranch, and how it is that I access the property. He established this contact through email. Soon after, we became friends. Through our conversation, I learned that he was becoming disenfranchised with employment at the ranch. Perhaps it wasn't all it was cracked up to be.

Regardless, he started out by telling me he was fellow researcher and had been out to the Ranch a number of times. He asked me if we could meet out there so I could show him different ways to get on the property. Of course, I was somewhat suspicious and suggested he contact someone more local instead. He contacted me again two days later, telling me that he was up on the mesa from where he spotted not only the balls of light but also a creature of sort moving in an out of the old homestead. I didn't hear from him again until a week later. That was when he told me he actually worked security on the property, but that if I kept things quiet, he would be willing to help me out.

At the time I was also in the process of moving residences. I expressed to him the stress I was under to get out of one house and into the other, and he offered to come up and help me move. He made the trip up to Wisconsin, and we spent about a week hanging out. It was during this stay that he told me about his military background and the connection between BAASS and the type of security they hired. Ultimately, he did share with me some of his own experiences on the Ranch, tell me about some of the security procedures, and provide me with other sources of information I may not have had access to otherwise.

FORUM QUESTIONS

As part of the podcast program, the host, Gene Steinberg, was taking questions from the live forum. Some of them were more interesting than others, the gist of which are presented here.

GOLD COINS

One of the listeners brought up a question about Terry Sherman and his son finding a 19th century gold coin there on the ranch and seemingly in pristine condition. As the rumor goes, as soon as they picked it up, it immediately tarnished and aged right before their eyes. Although I had never heard this story, Steinberg confirms that Sherman himself told him about the incident. Sherman swore to him that when he found that coin it appeared as if newly minted. He also told Steinberg that he was still in possession of the coin, and it was there in the house. Steinberg, though, never asked to see it, certain that the opportunity would arise at another time. He had not expected that

Sherman would sell the house to Bigelow within a couple of days of his visit and he would never again be permitted access to the property. As for the coin, he references similar stories told by others who finding gold coins in the canyon further north experienced the same phenomena.

DARK CANYON

There was also a question about Dark Canyon and its location. At this point, I reminded the listening audience that I have, at great peril, done things out there which I would not recommend to others. By peril, I mean that much of the land in this territory is Reservation land and under the jurisdiction of the Indian Council. Trespassing is highly discouraged and trespassers are not dealt with kindly. Dark Canyon happens to be one of those places. It is taboo to the tribes; they don't go there. It is also forbidden to outsiders, such as myself. One of the reasons for this taboo, according to Junior Hicks, who was told as much from tribal elders, is that Dark Canyon is considered to be the lair of the Skinwalker. I risked much by going there—not only arrest, but making of myself persona non grata and falling into disfavor with the locals and the council.

IS THIS ALL REAL?

I was asked by one of the listeners if I felt the search creates the events, or if the events have always been out there, and by searching we actually encounter them. In other words, as researchers do we invent our discoveries? While it is perhaps a product of both, meaning we go out there looking for paranormal events but we do so in locations where they are most reported, I do not believe I am in any way creating or fabricating these encounters to fit my expectations. The simple fact is, you can't expect to sit home on your recliner and have these events come to you. In addition, if you choose to ignore the possibility that the paranormal is real, you'll have no reason to discover otherwise. In my case, I believe there is more going on around us than our everyday existence suggests, and as such, I have made it my personal mission to find out as much as I can. For me, the Ranch provides that opportunity.

For those less familiar, the ranch is not the only hot spot in that area. There are at least two similar and well-known locations in Colorado, both of which Bigelow attempted to purchase. The first is in Black Forest, Colorado. The second, known as the Evans' Ranch, is in Elizabeth, Colorado. The Evans' place is rumored to be haunted and was featured on the TV program *Fact or Faked*. It has a reputation for strange events and anomalies, and is located in an area well-known for cattle mutilations. In the snippet of an email from 1996 that I have read, the owner referred to Colonel John Alexander, the former director of NIDS, saying that Alexander was trying to get into his head, telepathically, to brainwash him into the sale. He also infers there were threats against his family, but doesn't state by whom.

THE ENTITIES

The question here is are we dealing with multiple entities in this environment, or is there a single entity manipulating perception? Speaking to other investigators, there is strong belief that this activity is related to some kind of military psychological operations. For me, that is just a little too much conspiracy. I believe there is a single source, both ancient and spiritual. It is dimensional, meaning a physical realm which exists parallel and in proximity to our own. The theory to which I prescribe is the basin, and perhaps much of the Four Corners territory, is a place where whatever force it is that separates these two dimensions is least prohibitive, allowing for these entities, which I believe to be four dimensional, to cross into our world at will—or at least some manifestation of them.

Asked as to why I reject the military or government conspiracy aspect of it, I answer that we as humans don't turn into balls of light or wolves. I don't believe in magic. Therefore, it seems rational to believe there could be other life forms out there with which we are not familiar.

As for the constant appearing and disappearing of these entities, while I am not a physicist or a scientist of any sort, the more I read about anything related to a higher dimensions, I have come to theorize that as four dimensional beings, when they appear here in a three dimensional environment, they manifest as nothing more than a blob of light—a three dimensional representation of a four dimensional being. To better conceptualize the theory, consider how our own shadows appear: a two dimensional representation of a three dimensional body, and without mass or substance. As these four dimensional beings cross the dimensional divide— through the portal, they too surrender a dimension. The form that manifests, these balls of light, are then really only a reflection or silhouette of the actual beings. As they then cross back through the portal, as a four dimensional being, we can no longer see them. They disappear, as it were. Although I have no evidence to support this theory, the general makeup of the scientists on the Bigelow team seems to suggest there is something to the concept of portals and alternate dimensions.

THE MEYERS

One of the contradictions often referred to by the skeptics is whether or not the Meyers, the owners of the ranch prior to the Shermans, ever experienced any of the anomalies or incidents claimed by the Shermans. According to Frank Salisbury, the author of <u>The Utah UFO Display: A Scientist's Report</u>, the Meyers told him they never experienced anything out of the normal while they were there. My take on it is that they were convinced by Salisbury, who had an agenda of his own, to downplay or deny their experiences. As support, Salisbury was criticized by Gwen Sherman for the way he conducted the interview he had with her husband, throughout which he insisted on interpreting the family's experiences in a way that fit his own idea of what happened. It is worth mentioning that Salisbury has strong religious and Christian convictions.

As for whether or not the Meyers had such experiences, Steinberg himself, who was inside the ranch house, verifies the reports made in other publications that there were an inordinate number of locks and deadbolts within the house, suggestive of an intent to keep potential intruders from getting any further into the house, and that there was, if not in the traditional sense, a panic room in the heart of the home.

Two other interesting facts: The first is that the Shermans were directed not to dig on the property, which some researchers theorize was due to an observable increase in paranormal activity whenever the ground was disturbed. However, I was informed that it was because a son of the Meyers who died as a result of a horseback accident is buried there on the property. The second is that there is an Indian burial ground up on the ridge line.

WHY ALL THE SECURITY?

The presence of such extreme security would suggests something is being guarded. If so, what is it?

I have heard the security measures are there as a liability measure. The concern is that somebody trespassing illegally upon the property might fall, suffer an injury, and then seek to take legal action against the property owners. There is also the idea of the power lines overhead no longer being properly insulated providing for the fear of accidental electrocution.

However, I believe there is another form of intelligence out there, and that the security is well aware of it. As for being armed, it is both to intimidate and deter potential trespassers, and for personal protection. There is rumor, unverified, of an incident occurring in 1999 which resulted in either the accidental death or death by mutilation of an individual or individuals working on the Ranch. While Gene, who was told the story, has no evidence to back up the details, he does suggest that the denial of the incident provided at the time by Ranch officials left room for questions.

The version of the incident as it was told to me has to do with portal technology. According to the source, the ability to move through these portals is at times interfered with or disrupted by either the power lines or geomagnetism in the underlying rock. One of these portals opened unexpectedly and in an area directly above the head of one of the guards. This creature, tall and bulky, fell out to the ground. The guard, who was startled and frightened, opened fire on the entity—a reaction due to his training, and was in response killed by the creature. Ultimately, it was all a matter of miscalculation. I was told by Junior Hicks, and he from Bigelow, that these entities often have trouble navigating the portals while phasing in—that's what he called it, often entering off target, for example closer to Bottle Hollow or Fort Duchesne, and then have to make their way back to the ranch. They are not infallible.

In a similar story, Terry Sherman allegedly told Gene Steinberg of one of these portals opening out in front of the ranch house, which he is supposed to have seen multiple times, and out of which routinely came these triangular crafts floating gently. However, this one time, the craft then took off at high speed, too low, and sheared off the top of a row of cottonwood trees. Steinberg claims to have seen the trees, all slashed off neatly at the top.

THE PARACAST—the Gold Standard of Paranormal Radio, June 29, 2014
With
Gene Steinberg and Chris O'Brien

This third interview with the Paracast took place following the publishing of my second book, Skinwalker Ranch: No Trespassing, which I wrote along with D. L. Wallace. Wallace's primary mission was to reign me in with regard to some of the criticism concerning the writing style in Skinwalker Ranch, Path of the Skinwalker. However, the two books are polar opposites as to objective. Whereas my first book is presented from a personal perspective, with the desire to convey what I was feeling while in the moment, this second book focuses on investigative reporting and the first-person narratives of others with similar encounters.

THE OPENING

I shared with Gene Steinberg and his audience that I have since expanded my interest in the paranormal to include the entire Uintah Basin area, which I have found to be a rich source of narratives and first person encounters. While my initial assumption, and of other researchers also, is that the Ranch is the location of a portal, a sort of rift in time or space or a multi-dimensional worm hole, I have since discovered the Natives, in fact, believe there are multiple portals throughout the canyon, and that they are all in some way connected.

This area, known by many as the Four Corners, was historically the lands of the Anasazi and the Pueblo Indians. While today, most people associate the expression with the point at which Colorado, Utah, Arizona, and New Mexico meet, the Natives have a more spiritual interpretation. For these people, the number four has deep significance, part of which is derived from the four cardinal points. As such, to them the Four Corners is actually the lands encompassed by Mt. Taylor (New Mexico) to the south, Blanca Peak (Colorado) to the east, Mt. Hesperus (Colorado) to the south, and the San Francisco Peaks (Arizona) to the west.

As to the question as to whether the presence of the Native Americans attracted the opening of these portals, or whether or not the portals were created by the Native Americans, either in actuality or an element of their mythology, Chris O'Brien is of the opinion that at best they may have stumbled upon them, but due to their spiritual nature, would actively avoid them. To support this position, I have spoken to several members of the Ute tribe who have told me of traditional roadways in the desert, which when traversed, seem to deviate of a sudden from their direct path to go around what would appear to be very passable terrain. This circumvention or deviation is to avoid portals. In fact, I was told that if it is portals I seek, the best way to find them is to go out upon these roads and look for the deviations.

An interesting side note and a story: There are local Ute who say that the property upon which the Ranch sits was at one time part of the Uintah-Ouray Reservation, but was sold due to the presence of one of these portals, and therefore considered taboo by the tribe.

To substantiate the connection, one of the members of the Sherman family told me of an encounter up on the mesa with an Indian, ancient in appearance, which seemed to materialize out of thin air. He appeared equally as startled by the presence of the eyewitness as the eyewitness was by his. In a similar story, one of the Ute speaks of an ancient Indian appearing among a number of these balls of light, out of the midst of which appeared this black swirling mist or fog, which then materialized into a multi-tentacle creature. He refused to say anything more about it, fearing that by doing so he would draw the attention of dark spirits to himself.

STRANGE FEELINGS

Gene Steinberg, who has not been out to the Ranch or the surrounding area personally, expressed curiosity as if there is a palpable sense or feeling to the presence of entities. I believe a person's mind set makes all the difference. An individual with an open mind is more likely to be sensitive to this energy. One who is skeptical is less likely to feel the presence. My advice is to go out there alone, find a far off mesa which is isolated, set up a tent and a folding chair, wait for night to settle, and then go along for the experience. Given the high frequency of paranormal events in the region, the odds are good that you are going to see or encounter the manifestation of something that will have you questioning some of your beliefs. But be warned. As O'Brien says—and he has done quite a bit of fossil hunting out in those canyons, the Uintah Basin is just plain creepy.

For those who may be considering taking the trip, keep in mind that permits are needed to go on reservation land; they can be obtained from local offices. For those who are more interested in the Ranch, there is a creek that runs along the edge of the property which you can walk along. However, that too may require the obtaining of permits from the Bureau of Land Management.

I myself have been in these areas, but have limited my trespassing on any private property, including the Ranch. And while I opt not to talk about any unlawful encounters I may have had personally with Ranch security, I am aware of a fellow researcher who was pursued from the Ranch and out into the desert—guns were involved. He was fortunate, managing to escape over difficult terrain and into the rocks, and this due only to his familiarity with the landscape.

SECURITY ENCOUNTERS

Many of the locals, as do I, refer to the Ranch security as armed mercenaries—bored by the routine and waiting for something to happen so they can pull their guns. It is considered a potentially volatile situation. That said, the rumors regarding their activities are generally exaggerated. As to my own personal experiences, I have had the opportunity to speak with a number of them, at times separated only by the property gate or fence, and have found they are generally down to earth and amenable to conversation.

While most interactions with the guards are limited to trespassers at or near the gate, and the occasion on which the gentleman used his car to pull down the gate, the one that surfaces most has to do with a caravan of black, tinted-window SUVs. What makes these eyewitness encounters particularly of interest is that no one ever sees them going onto the property, only coming away from it. This is suggestive of there being some other means by which to access the Ranch, which to some may be subterranean.

One other story speaks of individuals who in their vehicle drive away from one gate and towards the other, only to find themselves suddenly surrounded by security vehicles.

In addition, in conversations that I have had with others who claim to have accessed the property, there is the one constant of hearing the muffled sound of a helicopter overhead and the sound, as if through a bullhorn, of commands being barked. Besides the clandestine arrival and presence of the helicopter, there is the question as to where it originates from given that the nearest airport is in Vernal, well to the north.

In a related story, some of the locals speak of having seen a large flatbed truck coming from the ranch and carrying some object which was concealed beneath a canvas tarp. There was also said to be at least one helicopter present in the air above the ranch at the time and more than one of these black SUVs. The locals who were there were then approached by police—not property security, who in response to their curiosity told them that a local resident committed suicide. They assumed by all of the activity that the incident occurred on the ranch. Later, when BAASS officials were asked to comment on the report, there was vehement denial that any death of any sort had occurred on or in relation to the property, despite the comment by local police. In addition, Gene Steinberg, the host of the Paracast states that he has spoken directly with two reliable sources, both of whom confirm the death.

Due to reports and rumors of this nature, the general consensus is that the NSA or the Department of Defense are somehow involved with Bigelow and the Ranch. While I have been able to obtain numerous documents from a variety of sources, none of them make specific reference to either one of these entities. Regardless, I have to admit, even if they did I would be reluctant to reveal as much, wishing not to make of myself a target of Federal interest.

While such concern may appear on the surface to be paranoia on my part, I have already had suspected Bigelow plants insinuating themselves into the forum on my site, www.SkinwalkerRanch.com. Their efforts have been limited to trying to discredit me and the information I share with the community, but it is an indication of how far those involved in maintaining the secrecy of Ranch activities will go to discourage the dissemination of information.

CURRENT EVENTS

Despite rumors to the contrary, including speculation by Steinberg during this broadcast, Robert Bigelow does still own the Ranch. I have checked with local realtors, and Bigelow properties is still the owner. As to anything more current on Bigelow himself, other than his continued work with his space stations, the most advanced model of which is scheduled to launch some time in 2015, there are no significant developments with regard to his direct involvement with the Ranch.

The dog-man story, which my second book, <u>Skinwalker Ranch: No Trespassing</u>, details extensively, has been confirmed by multiple local sources and has received media attention, not only in the local newspapers, but on various paranormal programs, including the Paracast.

For those who haven't had the opportunity to read about it firsthand, Bigelow dispatched two investigators, Joel Logan and Paul Jantzen, both with extensive law enforcement backgrounds, to investigate the sightings by locals of an upright canine-like creature which was moving about neighborhood yards, peering in through windows, scaling up the sides of houses, and leaping from roof to roof. One family claimed the creature came up to their corral, scaring the animals. When the man and his stepson went out to investigate, they were near overcome by the odor of death or rotting flesh and an unexplainable sense of dread. They then caught a glimpse of this creature as it fled into the nearby trees. Following up on the incident, Logan and Jantzen tracked the creature towards the creek out by the Ranch property, and they did manage to collect hair samples and cast a molding of its footprints. The creature has since been spotted by numerous other locals. However, to this point, the police have had no success capturing the creature and no one has managed to take a credible photo, although some local teens were said to have cellphone video.

As for the metal rod which was alleged to have been found on the property and in proximity to a mutilated calf, the last I heard it had been sent to BAASS for analysis. The results of the tests, at least from what I could discover, revealed the rod was made from element 115, which is not found here on Earth. Coincidentally enough, items of this same metal were associated with Area 51. I am aware the Junior Hicks, who was initially in possession of the rod before handing it over to Ranch scientists, has since requested its return, but has received no response.

OTHER PORTALS AND AREAS OF INTEREST

Mentioned fairly extensively in my second book is an airfield in Tyler, Texas, just north of Houston and not too far from the Louisiana state line. The one-time owner of a building along the air strip has been communicating with my routinely as to his experiences out there. From what he tells me, it is quite possible that there is a portal upon the property, which at one time had belonged to a local tribe and had been part of the reservation. Like the property in the Uintah Basin, it too was considered inhabited by dark spirits and held as taboo. It was at a later date sold to the county, and was shortly thereafter converted to a single runway airfield. The individual who has been communicating with me reports seeing frequent light anomalies, UFO aircraft, strange beings, and a dog-man similar to the one spotted in and around the Fort Duchesne area. I plan to go out to investigate these phenomena by the end of the year.

Satan's Butte in Arizona is another area of interest. It lies dead south of Skinwalker Ranch, reminiscent of the concept of the lay lines associated with paranormal settings in Europe. There is also a ranch in Buckley, Arizona. Bigelow's team was involved in researching both locations, and it is assumed they suspect there are other portals here, too. The Bradshaw Ranch is another fascinating place. I have been there multiple times and have had encounters, which may or may not be portal related. The government took over the property from the owners and fenced it in. Security, however, is not as intense as on the Ranch in Utah. I hopped the fence—as have others, including Chris O'Brien, and spent the night out there on a high point where the ruins of an older structure remain. While there, I saw three glowing triangles in the sky, translucent, in the sky above the ranch house. Indian Wells, upon the Navajo reservation in Arizona, is also a place of interest. Hominids, such as Bigfoot or Sasquatch, are a common sighting on the reservation.

WHAT NEXT?

Since publishing my second book, my real-world occupation has given me the opportunity to drive throughout the United States, and particularly the south-west. During this time I have made it my mission to speak with the local folks, especially Native Americans inhabiting the Four Corners, to encourage them to share with me any insight they may have as to the paranormal or any encounters they may have had in the first person, or may have been experienced by people close to them. The final section of this book is dedicated to these people.

CONVERSATION WITH LOCAL RESIDENT & RANCH NEIGHBOR

I had an interesting conversation with a resident living the past 32 years in the vicinity of the Ranch, meaning practically next door, which started on December 7, 2014. Her name is Janice and she reached out to me based on the negative impression she had of some of the contributors to my website forum. She found them to be less than authentic, and in some cases comical. She even went so far as to say, "The interview with that one person is a joke, stuttering around and having no idea what he was talking about." She found the details he was providing as not inclusive of "true and verifiable facts".

Initially I was under the impression she was talking about me. But after she clarified her message, I acknowledged there is extensive misinformation associated with the Ranch, much of which I believe can be attributed to overly active imaginations. I then asked if she had any encounters or experiences she might care to share.

UFO IN FORT DUCHESNE
In response, Janice starts by making reference to an incident which occurred in Fort Duchesne on February 12, 2012, at approximately 6:00 AM on the Uintah-Ouray Reservation. According to a witness named Corey, he and a co-worker are in their place of business when suddenly the power goes out. He, the co-worker, and a client go outside and notice bright red and blue lights flickering softly from behind a building south of their location. The lights then start blinking faster and more brightly. Together they head towards the light, laughingly thinking they are dealing with a UFO. As they near the location, they see a ship they believe to be a definite UFO, and definitely not a satellite or something recognizable. All three are excited and scared. However, in the name of safety they make the decision to go back inside the building, Corey afraid of abduction. They re-enter the building and put the doorstop in place to secure the inside. Suddenly the light turns green across the snow. It flashes brightly, as if a flash bulb. There is then a snap of light and they are enveloped in total darkness and pure silence. Corey insists this particular encounter was not his first, that he has had others while living in Randlett and while driving through Fort Duchesne. The encounter is further verified by other witnesses.

Janice then goes on to acknowledge that she and three other families live in proximity to the Ranch. She refers to it as UFO Ranch. She insists that strange and unexplainable occurrences are a routine part of living in the area, many of which she describes as mind blowing. She says that she and her neighbors prefer not to speak of these incidents as to not encourage curiosity seekers, the number of which when UFO sightings become public flock to the area and interrupt the life of the residents. She mentions that she had watched an interview with a local named Larry C., and that it was he that informed her that I was the person to contact if she wished to speak about the phenomena.

At this point, I again ask her if she has had any direct contact with any UFOs or paranormal entities, making a general reference to chilling stories shared with me by the Myers, John Garcia, Charles Wynn, and others, all neighbors living in and around the area in which the Ranch is located.

In her response, Janice seems to confuse me with Ryan B., another researcher interested in the Ranch. Jack Osbourne, the son of Ozzy Osbourne, the one-time lead singer of *Black Sabbath* and successful solo artist, was the host of a program called *Haunted Highway*, which in 2012 did an episode on the Skinwalker. Apparently, Osbourne spoke with Ryan B. Janice also goes on to criticize Osbourne for taking his investigation into an area called the Bottoms, which from her reaction is not an active location for these types of anomalies. In addition, she confirms that both John Garcia and Charles Wynn are both reliable sources of information as to the Ranch and the phenomena. Wynn, who has since passed away, having died of a cancer related illness which may or may not be attributed to the environment there in that part of the state, is counted among Janice's good friends, and a man to whom her own children referred to as Grandpa Chuck.

As for Ryan B., he and I had worked together for a brief time, traveling out towards the Ranch together. I had initially made reference to our collegiality in my first book, <u>Skinwalker Ranch, Path of the Skinwalker.</u> However, that reference was removed at his request. I tell Janice about this book, and the second one; however, she professes no knowledge of either, or of any of the television or radio shows in which I participated.

NO HARM INTENDED

As our conversation continues, Janice says that people have the "wrong perception of what goes on down here." When she had her first encounter, she had to ask herself if it really happened. She does not, however, provide any details, other than to say she has become accustomed to such incidents. She then adds that if these entities, which again she does not describe, had intended any harm, they would have done so already.

At this point, I tell her about my encounter with the black mist which coalesced into the wolf, and I make additional reference to the fact that there had been others. With a sense of humor, she suggests that I perhaps was someplace I didn't belong. That place, of course, was Werewolf Ridge. I then shared with her my opinion that whatever the entities out there, they seem to me to be a sort of sentry or guard maintaining a vigilance over the area, and although I perceive them to be emotionally horrifying, I too have never been accosted physically or approached aggressively.

Somewhat going off the subject, Janice tells me of a couple who lived in the area a few years back, and who, she says, were involved in some sort of devil worship. She said the house in which they lived was often the source of "crazy music". In addition, people told her they saw burning crosses in proximity to the property, something she herself did not see. I, too, recall having heard similar stories. Eventually the home was abandoned, and Janice and her son took the opportunity to have a look. When she entered one of the rooms, she immediately felt a dark presence. She responded by pushing her son from the doorway, saying, "No, we can't go in there. It is evil."

Getting back to paranormal events more in keeping with the topic of our conversation, Janice relates an experience in which unexplained light anomalies "were hitting down real bad" out in an open field. These lights had no identifiable source. As a result, she called the police department. When the officers responded, they refused to go out into the field in which the lights were displayed, or even to take any photographs. She added that lights of this sort are a common occurrence. Responding to a reference about the voice or presence of a little girl—a description provided to me by others and often is association with these types of lights, she says that whatever it is "crashes through the trees" making a noise that "is certainly not a little girl". She refers to it as big.

I then ask her about a noise which Charles Wynn and his children describe as a "giant strum chord, like a guitar string". Janice answers that she, too, has heard the loud hum, and then goes on to suggest it may be related to UFOs. "We saw the biggest dang ship ever," she said. "It scared my daughter-in-law so bad she was crying." After this, she goes on to say that there is writing in the hills that only she and her sons—as well as Charles—know the location of. According to her description, the writing is not visible from above, that you have to go down into the rocks themselves to see it. The language is not English or, so she suggests, any language she recognizes.

I myself have been all through the area in and around Charles' property and do not recall having seen any such writing. I ask her if it is perhaps in a cave; I am aware there are small caves throughout the rocks. But she says the writing is out in the open—if you know where to look. It is her opinion the message is extraterrestrial.

At this point in our conversation Janice is required to plug in her phone in order to continue exchanging texts. She then tells me that "crazy stuff" routinely comes over the phone, and that the same occurs with her friends and neighbors. Some are so unsettled by the occurrences that they no longer call her and only text. I acknowledge that I, too, have phone problems whenever I am talking about this particular topic. She responds by saying, "Maybe they don't want you in the circle."

I answer, "They had me write two books and go on TV for some reason, and make me come back out [to the Ranch] all the time."

THE THREE DOGS

Janice says it is her perception that these entities have different needs from each person with whom they interact. She then segues into a story about her dogs, which she says was one of her earliest encounters. She says she had three black, shaggy dogs. They were out in the field barking, but she was too tired that night to go out chasing after them. Suddenly, the aforementioned lights started "hitting down in the field", as she says. Charles, apparently, saw them too—the lights. But he saw them not only lighting up the fields, but also Janice's house. He became frightened at the intensity, jumped into his vehicle, and drove off towards the safety of the town. When he returned later, presumably that morning, he discovered Janice's three dogs high up in the branches of a tree on his property. They were dead. He informed Janice, but as the animals were too high up to go and get, they were left there. Although she doesn't say just how long—suggesting perhaps a year, they remained without rotting out, eventually dropped back to the ground by some heavy winds. They were buried, as were two mares and two colts which had also been killed with in that time period—none of which rotted out either, and remained on the open ground without being disturbed by the wild life. She indicates that

Fish and Game were called, but after the first time refused to return, leaving the disposition of the animals to Janice and her boys.

Obviously curious for more details, Janice told me that all of the animals had their blood removed and were in a petrified state, meaning stiff and hard like rock. As for the entities, she states that they are most active from midnight to about two or three in the morning. She offered to allow me access to her property to attempt to capture this movement on video, but at the same time reminds me that it is tribal land, very extensive and open, and that activity on her property—populated by horses which might discourage the entities—may be different than activity on the property of her neighbors. She says, too, that she owns land "right back where they [the Ranch] have the lookout [bait pen] set up." I assume, and she confirms, that her property is west of the Ranch.

As Janice seems willing to be open about her experiences and impressions regarding the anomalies and entities, I ask her if she had ever encountered the black swirling mist, heard the disembodied voices, or seen the spot light without an identifiable source. She responds by saying, "They [often] hit us with their lights, let us know they're still here, and zoom by us." She adds that her husband found these brief encounters as scary as hell, but that she is not bothered. "I guess," she says, "because they have been around so much, nothing scares me about them." She also claims to have a significant amount of video verifying their presence, but that "it's put away someplace safe." She then references "people coming from Denver [that are] always trying to get things."

As I had recently returned from making a delivery in the Denver area, I ask her if she is talking about me, acknowledging that as well as an author I am also a truck driver. But she confirms that she has never seen me in her life.

Of course, I am curious about anyone else that may be investigating the related phenomena, and especially the Ranch. But she tells me she doesn't know who these people are, only that they travel in black vehicles—primarily SUVs—with deeply tinted windows. They came up to her property and without identifying themselves presumed to ask her questions about the activity in her fields. She sent them away without answering their questions and reminding them they were on sovereign land. They then attempted to corner her son. He too walked away from them. I shared with her that it is my opinion these individuals are military personnel traveling and operating incognito, and that they are in some way connected to the Ranch and some covert activity taking place in the area.

Janice then related an encounter she had with a member of Ranch security. He tried, according to her, to "push his weight around" and to present as intimidating with his firearm front and present. She, too, told him he was trespassing on reservation land, and that if he didn't leave immediately, she would call tribal police and have him arrested.

Janice also claims as a friend Jean Dietz, a one-time neighbor and friend, who is currently residing in the Ranch house and serving, along with her husband, as the caretaker of the property. Janice, however, makes the point that she never sees Jean anymore. I acknowledge, from my understanding, that Jean and her husband have a pretty good thing going, living in the house essentially free-of-charge and in exchange for the service.

At this point, Janice asks me if I am aware of a location called Sunshine Acres. I am not. She informs me it is an area known for its paranormal activity, and that it is located just east of UFO Ranch (the Ranch) and near to the property owned by John Garcia. There are houses both to the left and right, and this development is known as Sunshine Acres. It is here, she says, that she saw the wolf with red eyes. I assume she is talking about the wolf the Shermans encountered on their property when they first moved into the Ranch. She goes on to say that her oldest son, while driving back from Randlett one night and with others along with him, had his vehicle collided with by some creature wolf-like in form. Immediately following the incident, everyone in the vehicle was upset and scared, including one woman who actually went into shock. She also refers to Red Bridge and Hill Creek as being places of reported activity.

Hill Creek is approximately 100 miles south of Fort Duchesne and close to the area in which I had my first encounter while driving with Iryna to Las Vegas to get married. It is nearby to the Books Cliff area. She tells me it is here that people report the presence of a black car which drives along the heights of the ridge, a location which is impossible to access by car. She describes it as long, sleek, and with rounded rear lights, and says that her son has seen it too. I have also seen this car—a story I have not shared with anyone, but not up on the ridge.

A QUESTION OF VERACITY

I spoke again with Janice on December 13, 2014, at approximately 6:15 PM. Again I asked her about the lights, and whether or not she had seen them close up. I told her that although I had experienced the light in close proximity, I was in shock as a result and do not recall much in the way of detail. She says at first she thought it was just nosey neighbors. She went outside of her home to investigate and was bathed in the light. Although nothing happened to her, she does note that both her domestic animals and the local wildlife tend to avoid the spot over which the light settled, and that nothing grows there. She then says similar lights are often seen down in Randlett, supposedly in the vicinity of a back road alongside the cemetery, a place I know well and have been to. I have camped nearby during my investigative outings, and I am not afraid to say it is a scary place, especially in the dark of night.

I then challenged her, perhaps more bluntly then I had intended, relative to her claim of having knowledge of that extraterrestrial writing that she referred to earlier in our conversation. I in the interim had the opportunity to talk with some of the security guards I know, and who are familiar with that area, and they suggested there is no such writing anywhere about, other than the Masonic symbols which are known to anyone who has been there. In fact their exact words were "[she] wouldn't be able to tell where the writing is because it isn't real".

Janice, as I should have expected, became defensive, saying, "I thought you wanted to know the truth, but you just keep asking about the Ranch. Sorry, but I wish you the Very Best of a New Year."

Not wanting to discourage her and risk having her discontinue sharing with me, I changed the subject, asking her if she could tell me more about the black car and Books Cliffs, south of the Uintah-Ouray Reservation. It was in this area I took a photo of a strange looking car, but I'm not convinced it was the same one. She goes on to tell me that the car looks similar to the original batmobile, and that is appears only at night; she emphasizes that it has never been seen in daylight, but that other types—I assume she means ghost cars—have been witnessed. She assures me that if I go out by the ridge at night I will definitely see it as it is always there. To do so, she says, given the time of year, I will need a four-wheel drive vehicle capable of navigating the heavy snow.

I then ask her if she can point me in the direction of anyone who might be able to tell me more about the paranormal activity in the area. She mentions the old ones, by which she means tribal elders living out in the old homesteads. She says, however, that they are difficult to talk to as they are reluctant to deal with outsiders, but if I wish, they can be found by driving around a bit in the reservation and keeping my eyes open.

We again touched base late in January. I told her about a story I had just received from a man who had an encounter out by the ranch in which he was pursued by an entity which stayed just out of the line of sight but continued to make its presence known for more than the half-mile it took for him to get back to his truck from the place it first appeared. I asked her also if she had any experiences in which a bush or tree became animated and began to shake violently. She told me there was something roaming about the area not too long ago. The police responded and tried to say it was only a mountain lion. She, however, knew whatever it was, it wasn't a mountain lion or any other critter indigenous to the area.

Since our last conversation, I had asked if it was possible for me to come out there and visit her, take advantage of her knowledge and experience, and get the chance to move about her property. Hopefully we will be able to soon make these arrangements.

CONVERSATION WITH INSIDE INFORMANT

In February of 2015, I had a conversation with an individual who, among other things, has an intimate relationship with the previous owners of Skinwalker Ranch, as well as extensive knowledge of the area and its residents. This individual shared with me some inside information never before made public.

I started out our conversation with reference to an incident mentioned in an article by David Perkins written in 1997. According to Perkins, Terry and Gwen Sherman, the last night spent at the Ranch, awoke in the morning with their bed sheets soaked in blood and each with a "scoop mark" carved out of the thumbs of their right hand. I asked if there was any veracity to this claim.

The informant was unable to verify if this incident actually took place. However, she did acknowledge that the Shermans were under the impression that their time at the Ranch did contribute to some of the health problems they have experienced since they left. Again, no specific health problems were mentioned.

Personally, I believe that the balls of light, of which there is a strong presence within the area surrounding the Ranch, may be a contributing factor to the high incidence of cancer in the area, and as such, and due to the amount of time I have spent there, I have had blood work done. To this point, fortunately, I have no indication of any thyroid issues or other serious health concerns. Nevertheless, I maintain that Charles Wynn died due to exposure to these entities.

The informant then went on to say that the locals are convinced that the explosion of test bombs in the St. George area sometime back permitted fallout to contaminate the mountains and surrounding canyons. Supposedly, loggers working in the vicinity at the time reported silver colored cobweb like structures strung throughout the trees, which of their own accord, vanished but hours later. High incidence of illness followed, as well as the untimely and premature deaths of many of those workers.

The informant also furthered a theory I had no previous reason to entertain. She refers to what she considers to be an inordinate number of gay men in the area, suggesting that aliens may play a part. She says, "I can name about 30 [gay men] off the top of my head. I always wondered if the abductions were messing with the DNA, or the radioactivity levels affected the DNA." She also mentioned a high suicide rate, five of which, according to a friend of hers who works as a nurse in the hospital emergency room, took place in a single night.

    Furthering the conspiracy theories which abound with regard to the Ranch, the informant told of a knock on her door which occurred less than a few weeks prior to our conversation. When she answered, she was met by two gentlemen, one considerably older than the other. Both men were dressed casually and with no sign of affiliation with any government or official agency. The older of the two was in his 40s and appearing physically fit. He was wearing a white t-shirt, khaki-colored pants, brown polished loafers, and he was carrying a stack of papers, loosely gathered together and apparently without order. The younger man was in his early 30s. He had curly auburn hair styled above the ear. He wore a black t-shirt, black khaki pants, and black polished boots. He too had a stack of papers, held loosely with rubber bands. The older guy did all the talking. He asked the informant as to the TV service there in the home. The informant replied that she doesn't watch TV. He responded, "Okay, no TV." He then grabbed his soda cup from Arby's and left, his partner following behind. They didn't bother to introduce themselves, say who they worked for or represented, didn't shake hands, and made no attempt at small talk. "Didn't make sense," says the informant, "no flyers, no cards or handouts. [They left me] with a very uncomfortable feeling. [Perhaps I'm] being paranoid or something else. It's been a while since [my] intuition was so strong regarding something, and so bothersome."

    I then shared with the informant my experiences which suggest that the phenomena can and does manifest itself in forms other than wolves and birds. One of these forms is a men-in-black appearance, which I know for a fact has been experienced by neighbors of the informant. I then asked the informant if these individuals at her door were wearing glasses, did she happen to notice feet that were abnormal in size—she did get a good look at their footwear, or if they affected any curious mannerisms? She responded there were no glasses, but both had very large feet. She also said that the younger of the two presented like an excited puppy. He was behaving not like someone who was being trained, but as if he was trying to contain his emotions or intensity level. She also felt there was something not right about the papers they were holding, as if they were more a prop—thrown together and without any real purpose. The whole thing, she said, had an "odd feeling [that] something wasn't right."

For me, I've learned that the feet are a giveaway, that and the eyes. From the informants description I felt her visitors were more entity-like than military. I've had my run-in with that type, too. While I believe they have their interests in the area, they are quite distinguishable from the phenomena.

I then asked the informant what it was she believed they were after. She responded, "That's the million dollar question? What were they really looking for and why now? It's got me really concerned?"

As for her encounter with actual military men, the informant said she didn't learn much from them. One, however, was more open than the others and she found him to be credible. He told her—off the record—that military involvement and interest in the area, and the Ranch, went all the way to the top, insinuating then President Bush and the White House.

According to what this member of the government told her, the military obtained alien technology through "trade". They, meaning the military and the government, permitted the alien abduction of humans and the slaughter and mutilation of cattle free of consequence. People, after all, are plentiful and one or two here or there won't be missed. He went to tell her that there are "several different factions coming here from different universes. Some [are] good, some really bad."

In support of the informant, I was told by others close to the government—and of course confidentially—that the military learned much about the phenomena on Skinwalker Ranch from events in the 40s and 50s. Although I get only tiny pieces of information from which I have to extrapolate meaning, I have reason to believe the technology has to do with portals and perhaps the means by which to move from one alternative dimension to the other, or perhaps deep space travel here in our own universe.

In a final thought on the whole matter, the informant spoke about the activity of the scientist who were there on the Ranch. She said the impression by those closest to these scientist was that "what they were doing was not logical and [didn't] make any sense. [It was as if] they were trying to observe [the family] and the effect the phenomena was having on [them]." She then acknowledges, however, that feeling and facts are two different things, and that ultimately she and her neighbors were left with ever more questions and very few answers.

I concluded our conversation by asking her if she knew of or had ever heard anything about an old Indian named Mr. Marcus. It is my opinion that this individual may be one of these entities in human form. From what I've learned from others, he walks freely among us and has demonstrated supernatural abilities. I would also like to know if the Shermans really did awake that last day in the Ranch house with those wounds mentioned by the Perkin article.

As of now, I've yet to hear back from her.

RANCH PHOTO ALBUM

RANCH LAYOUT

MAP OF SKINWALKER RANCH AND SURROUNDING PROPERTY

   This map illustrates all of the key locations with regard to Skinwalker Ranch and the surrounding property. UFO Hilltop is to the upper left and is one of the preferred locations for getting a good look at the Ranch property. It is also situated on public land, so access is not a problem.
   This aerial view provides an accurate perspective as to the rugged and desolate landscape. Notice that the Hickens property is almost all stone and rock.
   The map also shows the approximate location of the Indian Burial ground (far right), and the cave just to the west. The property just to the east of the burial ground does not belong to the Bigelow property. The east gate is located just below this point on the ridge.

Bottle Hollow (pictured below), the reservoir which was constructed in 1970, is located directly north of the Ranch. It is here that the UFO was alleged to have avoided pursuing military helicopters and jet by disappearing beneath the surface of the water. Reportedly, the helicopters continued to circle the reservoir for a half-hour and then abruptly departed. Fort Duchesne is located just to the east of the reservoir, which is shown in the photo below. The reservoir, according to local lore, is also allegedly the home of a large black snake-like monster or creature responsible for the death of at least one person.

The area of the Ranch just to the south of the ranch house is one of the places on the property where the Shermans alleged to have seen a portal open up and an aircraft of some sort exit, as well as balls of light at other times. There is a second portal site by the Old Homestead to the west.

Below is a less detailed map, but one which gives perspective to the size of the ranch, the size of the Garcia property to the immediate east, and the properties to the southeast where the unidentified wolf-like creature was spotted and pursued into the tree line, and later investigated by two members of the BAASS team.

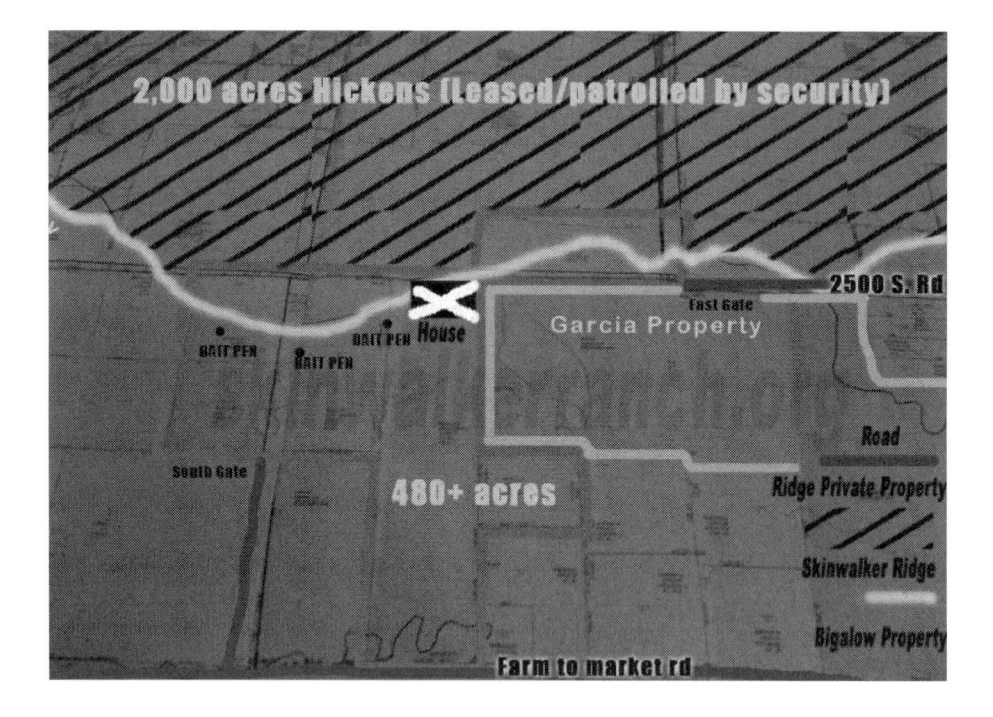

THE RIDGE

THE RIDGE (below the text)

This photo is taken from the ridge overlooking the ranch from the north. The ranch house itself is to the west (right) and the east gate, though it can't be seen from this perspective, is there at the base of the ridge. Looking to the upper left of the photo, just beyond where the shadow extends, is the pond on the Garcia property which marks the boundary between the two ranch properties.

This particular ridge runs east to west along the northern edge of the Ranch property, and actually makes up the north-eastern-most extent of the ranch. The property further north and to the west belongs to the Hickens, a wealthy gold mine operator who owns a significant amount of the land in Fort Duchesne. Sometime prior to 2010, Bigelow made arrangements with Hickens to include their property, at least in as much as it abutted the ranch, in the security patrol of the ranch personnel.

To the west of this ridge and at its base is the location of the abandoned homesteads referenced in Skinwalker Ranch: No Trespassing, and in the most recent book published by one of the ranch security guards, Lost on Skinwalker Ranch, written by Erick T. Rhetts. It is also in proximity to this area that many of the researchers interested in the ranch consider to be the most active in terms of the phenomena.

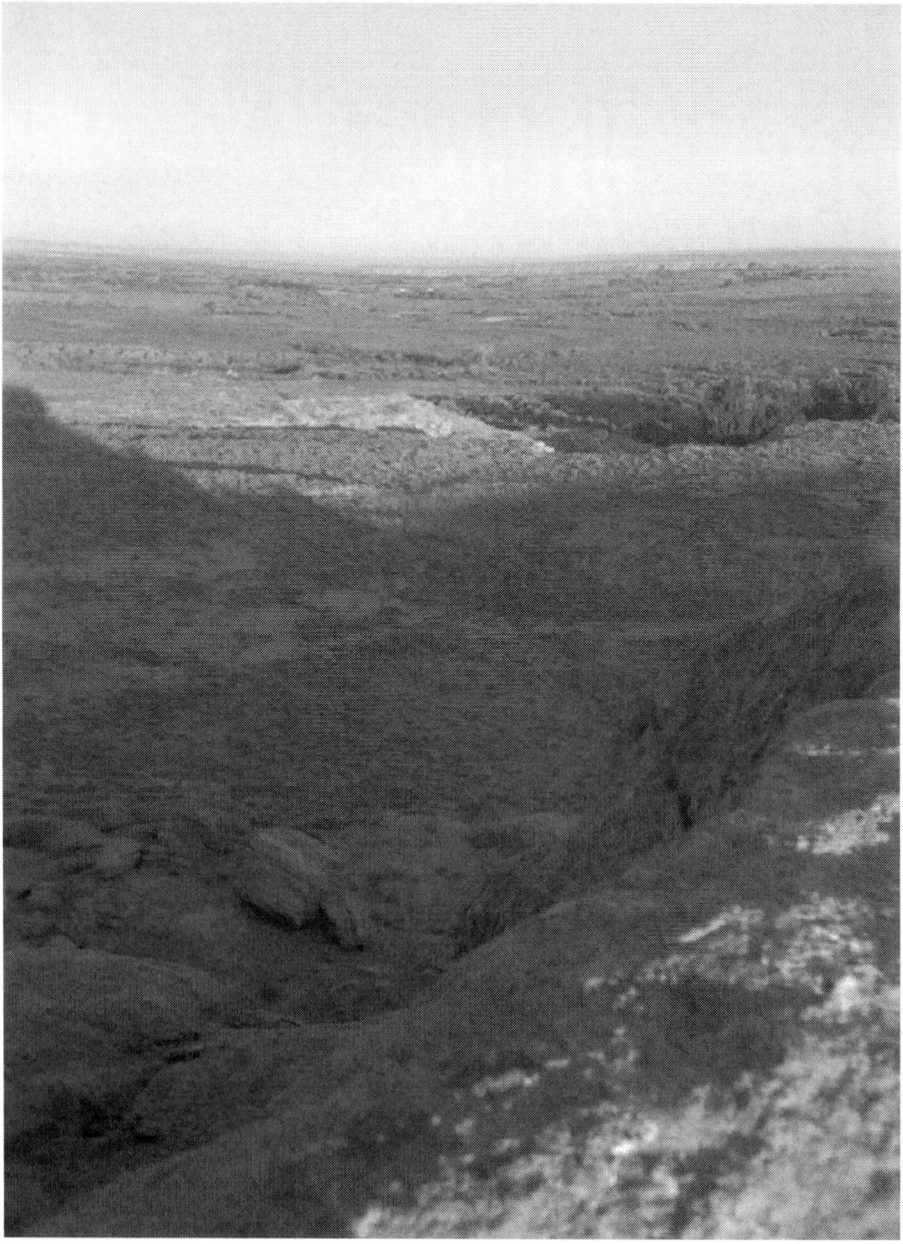

THE RIDGE (overlooking the fields)

This photo shows the view looking south south-west from the top of the ridge to the north of the ranch. The green expanse right of center is field three. The ranch house is to the left and out of the photo.

Through the center of the photo, and just to the left of the ridge rocks, is a dirt road that runs along the northern edge of the property. There to the right of the large copse of trees in the center, and showing as a dark horizontal cluster, is the old homestead. There is a second old structure within the copse itself. When I was first contacted by Chip, and he told me that he saw both balls of light and an upright figure coming from the homestead, this was the view that he allegedly had established.

NORTH RIDGE

While descending Werewolf Ridge, which lies just north of the ranch property and along the property belonging to the Hickens, I discovered a shallow cave, some ten to fifteen feet deep. (The cave is located in the middle of the red swirl.) While the existence of similar caves within the area is common knowledge, a fellow investigator, David Weatherly, the author of Black Eyed Children, reported having seen blue-colored orbs originating from this point. I believe from his description that they may have been coming from this very cave.

Though I am making no so such claim with regard to this particular cave, the people native to this area, and especially the Ute, often make reference to portals or openings which many believe spiritual or paranormal entities use to pass into this world from alternate dimensions. The Shermans in their interview with Zach Van Eyck speak of an experience in which they claim to have seen an aperture or opening in the night's darkness and from which came through a number of glowing orbs.

Due to its location on Ranch property, which is private and monitored by security, the cave, to my knowledge, has never been fully explored.

RANCH VIEW FROM THE SOUTH

This photo shows the ranch house from the south. The house can be seen in the middle of the trees slightly to the right of center. In the back ground is the ridge and the mesa. Most of this property belongs to Hickens, who sometime in 2009 agreed to allow the guards to patrol atop the mesa and on their property, further limiting access to researchers and other curiosity seekers. The field in the foreground is field number one and contains the bait pen in closest proximity to the house. The gulch is all the way to the fore and to this side of the trees. The Garcia property is all the way to the right, as is the east gate. The south gate is south of the gulch, which runs this side of the line of trees to the bottom of the photo. It is in this direction that the two investigators working for BAASS tracked the dog-man.

SKINWALKER RIDGE

This photo shows Skinwalker Ridge and just how highly elevated it is compared to the field below. As part of their patrol, the security guards were required to hike up to the top of the mesa. It was here that a fellow researcher was detected by the guards and pursued. However, by the time they were able to reach the spot where he was seen, the researcher was able to escape, making his way over and through a number of treacherous rock formations and eluding both the security and their dogs.

To the left of the photo, and in the middle of the green of the field, is bait pen number one. It is here that scientists were alleged to have secured a calf to present as bait to attract the entity that was thought to be slaughtering the cattle. The trailer in the corral can be seen to the right.

To the extreme left of the photo is the security pole which housed a security camera. According to a story related in the book by Knapp and Kelleher, the wires to that camera were ripped out and the camera rendered inoperable within a matter of fractions of a second, a feat for which human machination would be impossible, and for which, it is believed, some paranormal entity was responsible.

DRY GULCH

This photo shows the creek which runs to the south of the ranch. There are similar water ways which run close to other parts of the property. As these waterways are considered under the jurisdiction of the state, those seeking to get a close up look are known to wade into the water and approach the property without concern for trespassing. It may be possible to obtain a Fish and Wildlife permit to gain access to this creek.

This creek is also the one towards which the wolf-like creature described in Skinwalker Ranch: No Trespassing was pursued after scaring the family by coming up to the corral and house, and towards which led the footprints tracked by the two BAASS investigators. In addition, the creek is supposedly home to a creature the locals refer to as "water babies". These creatures mimic the sound of crying babies. When a person approaches to investigate, they leap from the water, grab the individual, and drag them below the surface to drown them. While I have not seen these creatures personally, I have heard the splashing of what I assume to be a large creature.

Perhaps it was only a beaver, but I was always too terrified to check for fear of being pulled in.

CAMPING SITE

This photo shows one of the camping sites at which other researchers and I stay while setting to investigate the Ranch and the surrounding area. The photo illustrates how foreboding the rocks are and how desolate is the location.

At night, the view of the surrounding landscape is breathtaking, the universe coming alive above our heads. During the summer, storms of heat lightning roll in and discharge bolts of electricity which add to the mystique and provide incredible theater. Dust storms and high winds are also part of the territory, and when it rains, the terrain and roads become non-traversable as the water pools atop the surface in a sort of soupy mud which can pull you down and trap you. On dry days, the air has a clean, crisp dusty smell.

Anyone considering to spend a night or two out there must be properly prepared, including the type of gear which protects against the elements—it gets very cold at night—and sufficient supplies, such as water and the kind of food which doesn't require refrigeration or effort to prepare.

The photo below provides a panoramic view of the desert just beyond the Ranch property. This type of scrub brush extends for miles in every direction, and outside of properties such as the ranch, there is very little cover from the sun and few fresh water sources.

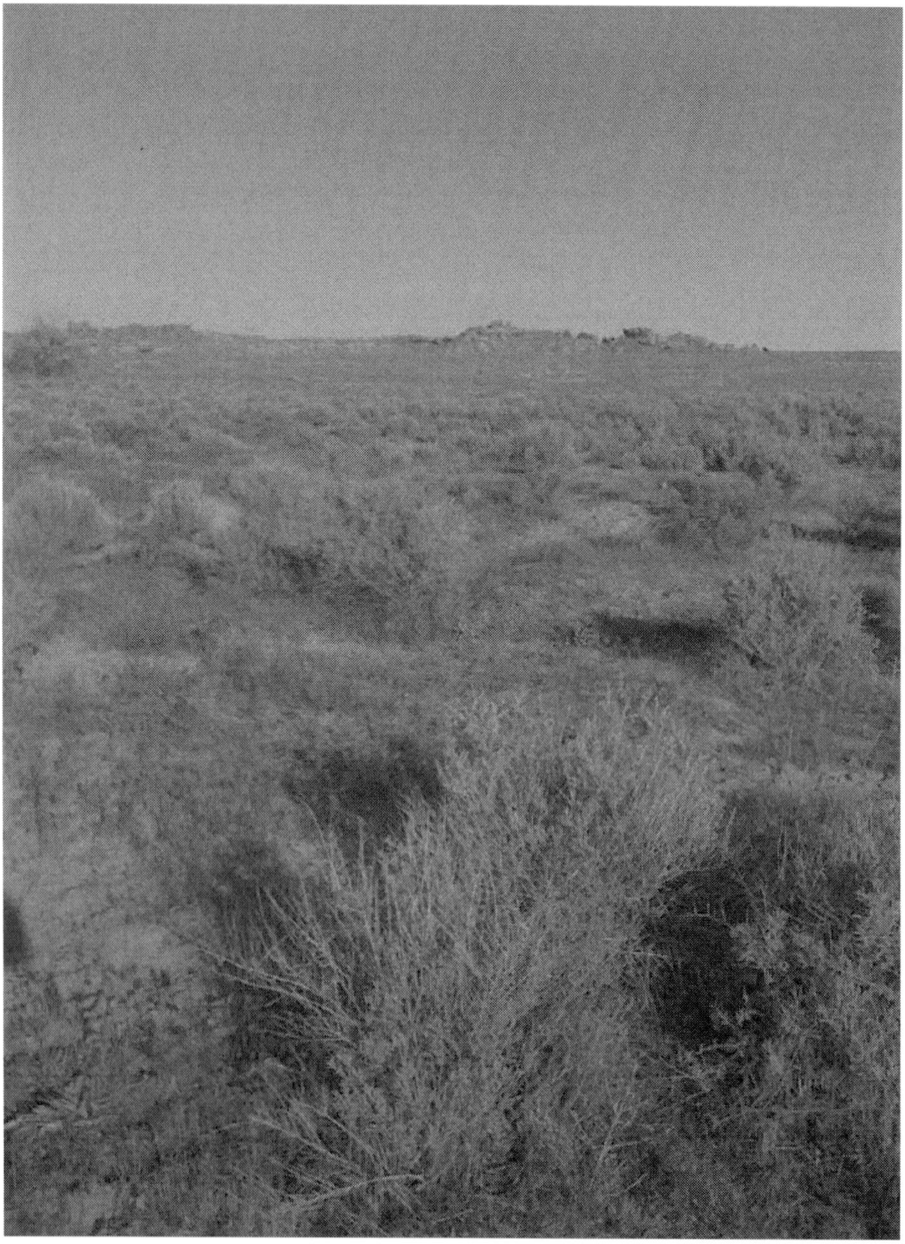

THE GATES

EAST GATE

There are two main gates to access the Ranch. The first is north-east of the ranch house, and to the north side of the road leading west from Interstate 80. It lies, more or less, across from the pond on the Garcia property, and leads to a dirt road that runs along the base of the ridge. The second gate is to the south and in proximity to the creek.

This photo is of the north gate and before the cement barriers were put in place. The ridge is seen in the background. Note the "Beware of the Dog" sign, which despite its ominous context, makes reference to canines which according to at least one security guard were little more than ranch dogs and typical pets. However, I have been informed by others that these dogs are, in fact, biosensors, trained to alert the guards to the presence of paranormal entities,

While trespassing on the ranch remains forbidden, the armed security guards contracted at the time of this photo were not connected in any way with the local police. They were directed by the property owner to chase off any unwelcomed visitor, and if trespassers were found on the property itself, to detain them until the local authorities were to arrive.

Nevertheless, there were strong rumors that the security guards would, if necessary, take matters into their own hands and deal with trespassers as they saw fit.

VIEW FROM THE SOUTH GATE

This photo shows the view from the south gate. The ranch house is to the left. The road coming in off of the county road and leading to the ranch house is to the upper right, beyond those tall trees. It is also from these tall trees that I would often see flashes of light, which insiders tell me is one of several portals opening. In the book by Knapp and Kelleher, mention is made of Terry Sherman shooting at a barely visible lizard-like creature which fell from these same branches. The extent of the ridge to the north, basically from the middle of the photo extending eastward and as far as the east gate is part of the Ranch property. The top of the ridge extending to the west is part of the Hicken's property.

ON THE RANCH PROPERTY

THE RANCH HOUSE

This photo—the only close-up view available—shows the front of the Ranch house. It is located in proximity to the east gate and in the shadow of the ridge to the north. After the Shermans sold the property to Bigelow and moved out, a couple by the name of Dietz moved in and became the caretakers. The wife Jean spoke of encounters and incidents she experienced, believing them to be paranormal. Her husband, John, however, remains adamant that nothing out of the ordinary has occurred during his time on the Ranch. The house has been renovated and remodeled since it was occupied by the Meyers.

THE OLD HOMESTEAD

This photo is a close-up of that horizontal cluster referenced in the previous photo. It is homestead 1, a structure that was abandoned prior to the arrival of the Meyers, and which to this day remains unused. It is in this spot where most of the paranormal activity takes place, and the most probable location of a portal. (A second portal, according to inside sources, is located to the top of the olive trees east of the Ranch house.) It is also here that the security guard referred to as Hobby Horse claims to have heard on multiple occasions the voice of the little girl who was allegedly killed at some time on the property, and where the dogs routinely become submissive. It is also here, according to the book Lost on Skinwalker Ranch, by Erick T. Rhetts, the security guard referred to as Riley encountered the two upright coyote-like creatures, after which he took refuge within, and allegedly stepped into the portal. It is also here that he was found almost three days later by other members of Ranch security.

INSIDE THE OLD HOMESTEAD

The photo above shows the inside of homestead 1. Riley's firearm was discovered between the rotted floor boards, yet there were no signs of him. The guards set watch, and despite their vigilance, he reappeared and was discovered during the change of shifts. No one saw him enter, nor were there any outward signs of his approach.

HOMESTEAD 2

Homestead 2 (photo below) sits across from the dirt road from the Old Homestead, which is also referred to as Homestead 1. Here in this small and dilapidated building is where the guards in Erick T. Rhett's book, <u>Lost on Skinwalker Ranch</u>, claimed to have followed the trail of two of the coyotes that had approached the Ranch house. The trail of these two critters led directly into Homestead 2 but did not come back out. When the guards then entered the structure, they found coyote footprints in the light snow settled there on the remaining floor boards. However, there were no other signs of the coyotes.

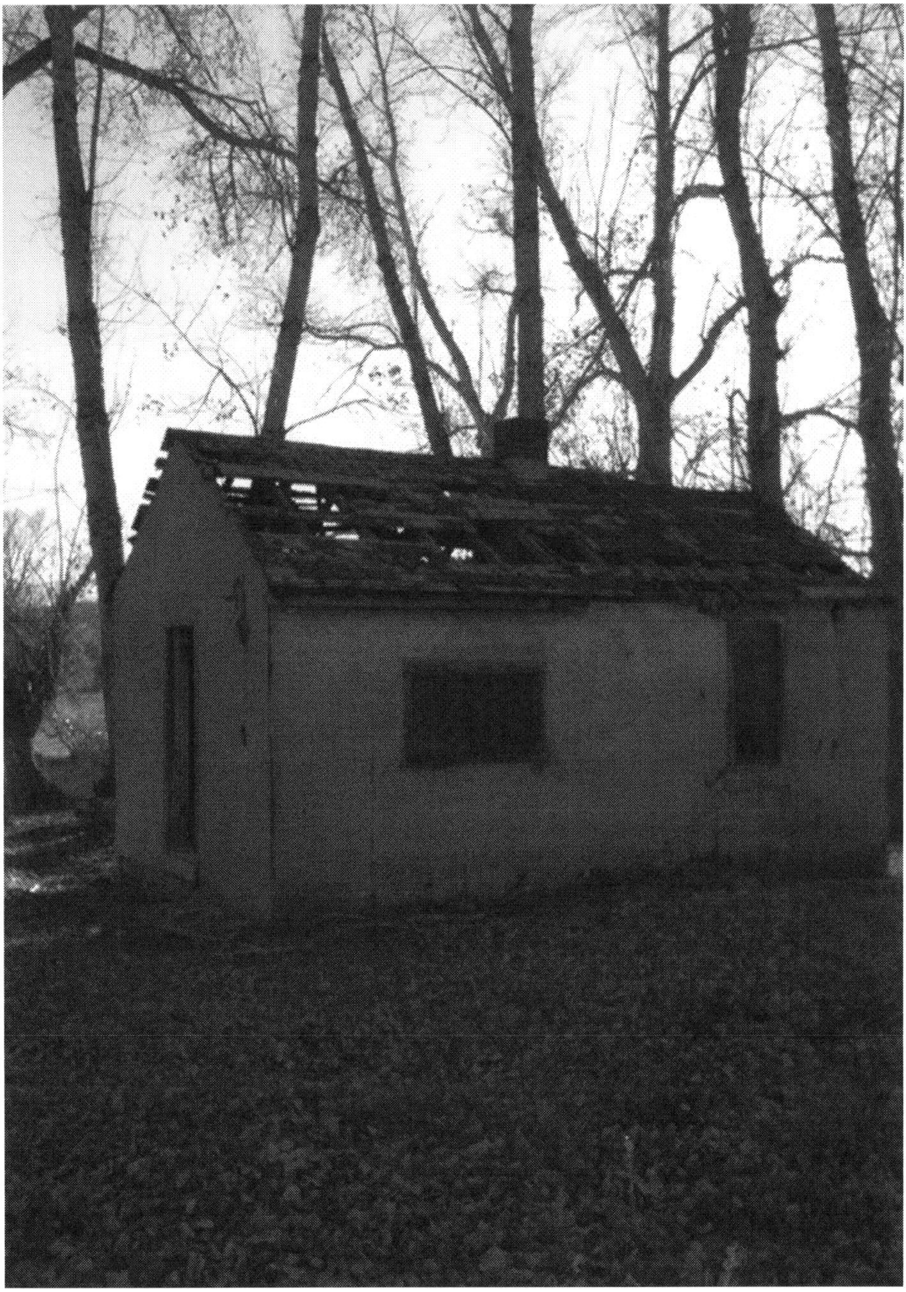

STORAGE TRAILER

This storage trailer sits in the corral to the north of the house and just below the ridge. There is only one story that relates to a storage trailer, and there is no certainty it is this exact trailer. At one point prior to selling the ranch, Terry and Gwen Sherman found a number of their prized bulls missing, and thought them to have escaped the corral and made their way out into the fields. Their search, however, failed to produce any hint of their whereabouts. Finally, having looked everywhere else, Terry turned to the trailer, a place the bulls would have had no way of getting into. Nonetheless, this is where he found them, crammed in as if they were sardines in a can. According to Sherman, the animals were in a state of hypnosis, and then suddenly, as if the spell was broken, they began to kick and struggle, causing extensive damage to parts of the trailer. How they got into that trailer remains unexplained.

RANCH VIEW FROM THE RIDGE

I am not going to say that this was the exact line of sight that we had when we encountered the Skinwalker, but it is close enough to provide a reasonable perspective. That night, we first saw the balls of light appear in an area in the fields just beyond those trees—our line of sight was somewhat higher and to the west, and then move towards the pole there to the right of the trailer to the left. It was from this trailer that security exited.

When the three balls of light made their way to our position, it was there beneath the rocks in the foreground that they first disappeared, and from which they then reappeared up and over our heads.

The dirt path seen to the right is the same one that leads from or to the east gate, and which runs along the base of the ridge. As it makes its way past the trailer in the corral, which is also to the right, it leads out to the old homestead buildings, and eventually to the western extent of the property.

RANCH HOUSE LIGHTS

This photo shows the Ranch house at night from the perspective of the ridge to the northeast. It is this very light that my partner and I were observing the night we had the encounter with the Skinwalker. One of the three spheres of light we observed swirled up the pole while the other two moved toward the roof of the house. Moments later, the light went out resulting in the exiting of the guards from their trailer. The guard was able to get the lights back on.

Charles Wynn once told me of a similar incident he experienced. He came home just around dusk to see several orbs of light fly towards the back of his house. They flew up to the transformer there in the backyard. Suddenly there was a shower of sparks and all of the lights in his house went out. Terrified, he put his car in reverse and fled to take shelter on a neighbor's property.

Just what relation these entities have with power sources, I can't say. However, they appear to radiate enough energy to overload the transformers, or perhaps drain them of the energy they produce.

BAIT PENS

Here is a close-up of the bait pens. It is obvious from the construction of the tower that its intent is to keep whoever is up and in it safe from whatever may be drawn to the area.

In some of the information I have read about the Ranch, these bait pens—of which there are three on the property—have been referred to as dog runs, suggesting contained areas in which the Ranch dogs can be contained and yet still have ample room to move around.

At first impression, this claim may seem valid, as the dogs were known to go after porcupines which are common in the area, and as a result suffer extensive harm from the needles. However, such rationale would preclude the need for barbed wire at the top of the fence, the long and relatively narrow configuration of the pen, and the relatively low height of the tower limiting the overall scope of view throughout the property.

Closer to the truth, then, is the claim that the pens were so configured to keep both the dog and researcher safe from the creature lured to the area just outside the pen by the calf secured by stakes to the ground and serving as bait. Notice that the barbed wire is angled outward to keep the creature from getting in.

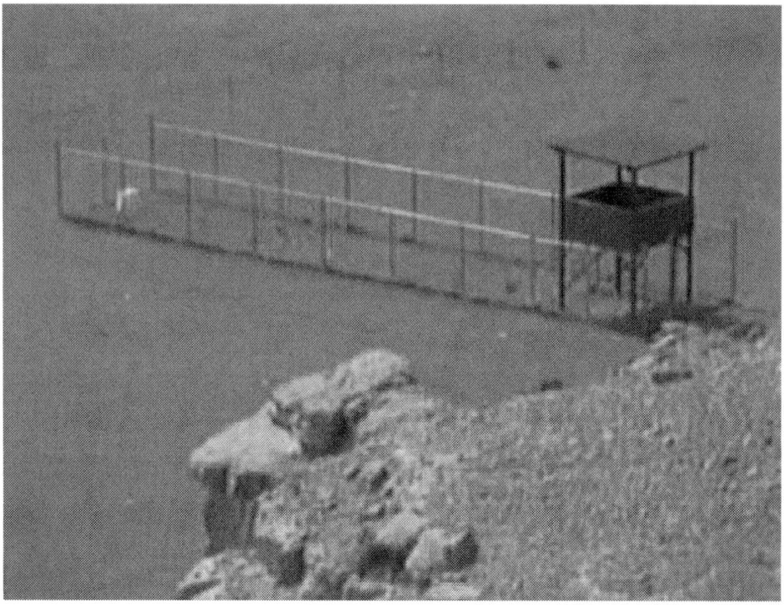

THE POWER LINES

These power lines, which run pretty much along the edge of the Ranch property, are the sole source of electricity to the entire area. These are the same power lines which seemed to come alive that first trip I made to the edge of the property, arcing and glowing and making a deafening noise.

According to one of my sources, these power lines have not been as well-maintained as one would expect given their significance, and their deteriorating condition is often given as the reason for discouraging people from venturing too close to the ranch. There is concern for random electrical discharges which may pose a hazard to anyone who is too close at the time.

As for the buzzing and arcing noises, they are unlike any I have encountered in my extensive travel throughout the United States. I contend there is something unique about them, and that there is a specific reason why these lines have been strategically placed around the Ranch.

This photo also shows the challenge the terrain presents to anyone seeking to make their way on foot from one place to another.

DRAWINGS AND OTHER RENDERINGS

BALLS OF LIGHT OVER THE RIDGE

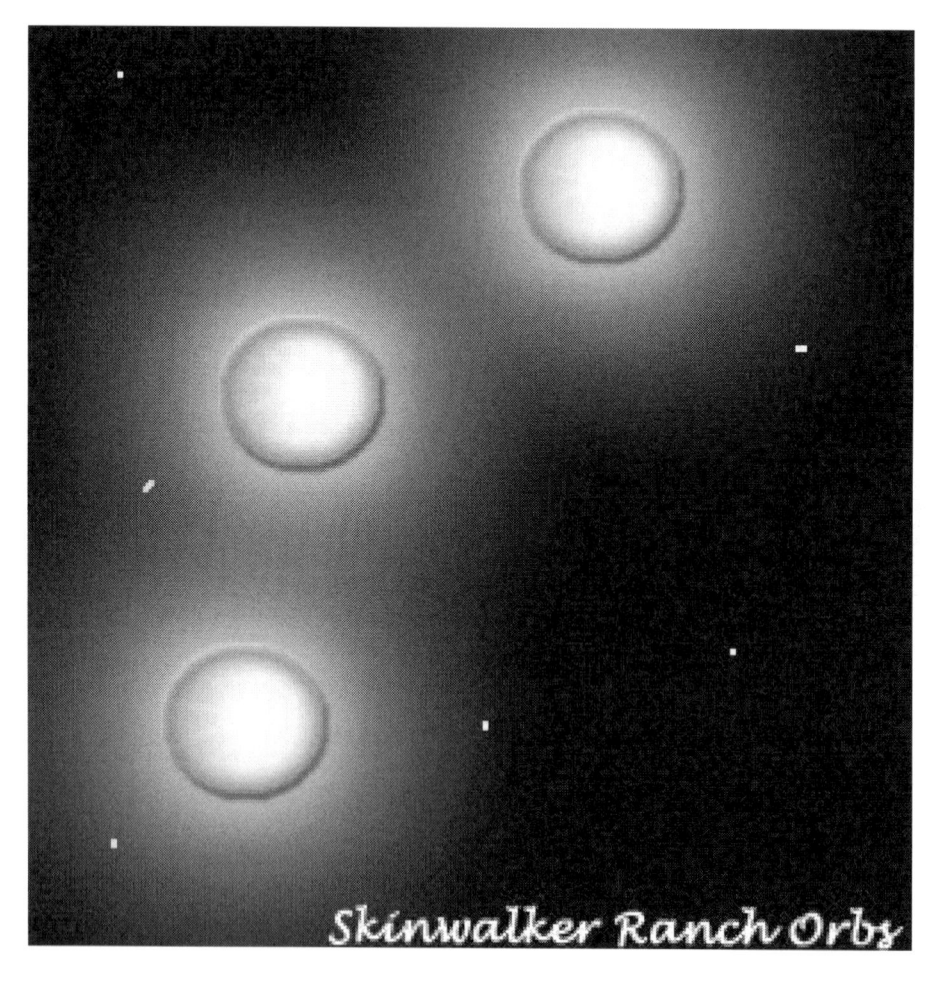

Skinwalker Ranch Orbs

    While this illustration and the one below pales compared to the real thing, it does give the reader an idea of the balls of light which appeared over our heads just prior to the encounter with the Skinwalker. They were otherwise noiseless, and would wink-out or power-down and become invisible to the naked eye. Sometimes, however, they would remain visible in the infrared of our night vision goggles. That said, they appeared not with any degree of structure, but instead as smokeless balls of fire or some sort of plasma. Their movement seemed intelligent.

As I provided in the narratives, both the other researcher and I had with us high-end video cameras. We were both recording simultaneously to obtain indisputable evidence of our encounter. When we left the area, we were certain that we had captured significant video files of not only these three particular orbs, but those that were moving about in the fields below.

I cannot describe my degree of elation knowing that we had captured indisputable evidence of paranormal phenomena which would lend itself to debate among skeptics and believers alike for years to come. Unfortunately, either our equipment malfunctioned or the entities themselves played a role in sabotaging our video files. Either way, we were left with nothing. We were crushed. Personally, I believe the material was eradicated when the orbs flew over our position and flashed light down upon us, thereby erasing the data. This depiction is the best I can do to at least help the reader visualize what it was we saw.

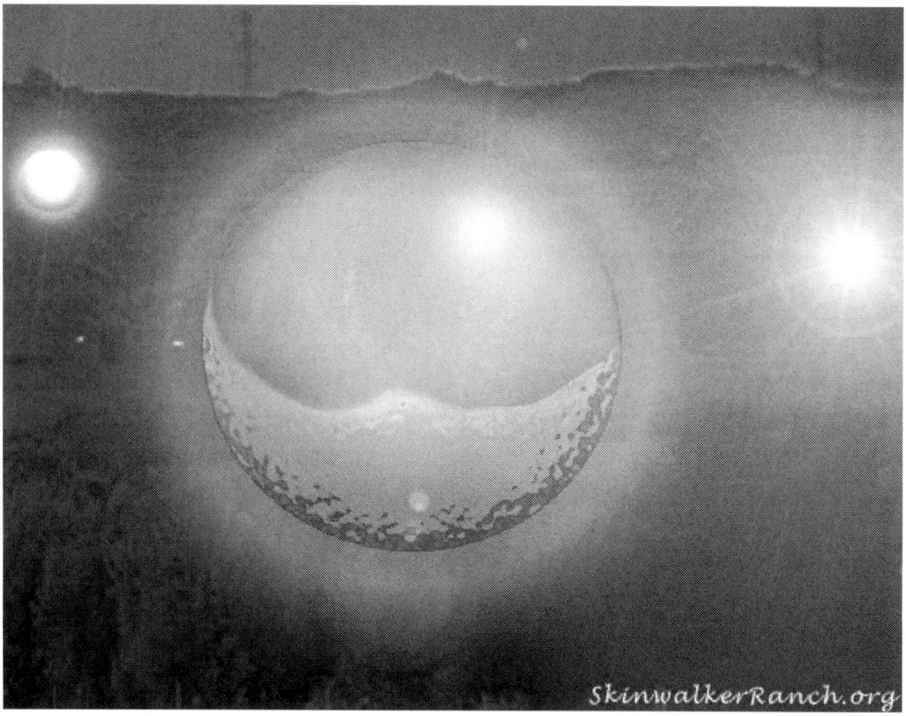
SkinwalkerRanch.org

THE PAPACROC CREATURE

Another paranormal investigator, and frequent contributor to the forum on my website, who refers to himself as Papa Croc claims to have had a disturbing encounter with a malevolent entity while he and two of his companions were camping in vicinity of the ranch. According to his recollection, he had stepped out of his tent late at night in order to relieve himself. Out of the dark rose this entity which robbed him of his sense of being, and in the process inserted through his nose and into his brain some type of bio-organism. It wasn't until later when he agreed to subject himself to hypnosis through arrangements with MUFON that he recalled the incident and his paranormal assailant. Greater detail is provided in my book <u>Skinwalker Ranch: No Trespassing</u>.

The above drawing depicts the entity's appearance. The elongated fingers, almost like tentacles, are considered a common trait of these entities, as is the pitch-black and mist-like to the body. The sketch includes the ball of light to the creatures back and from which it emerges. There are clear similarities to this sketch and the one made by the security guard, which appears below.

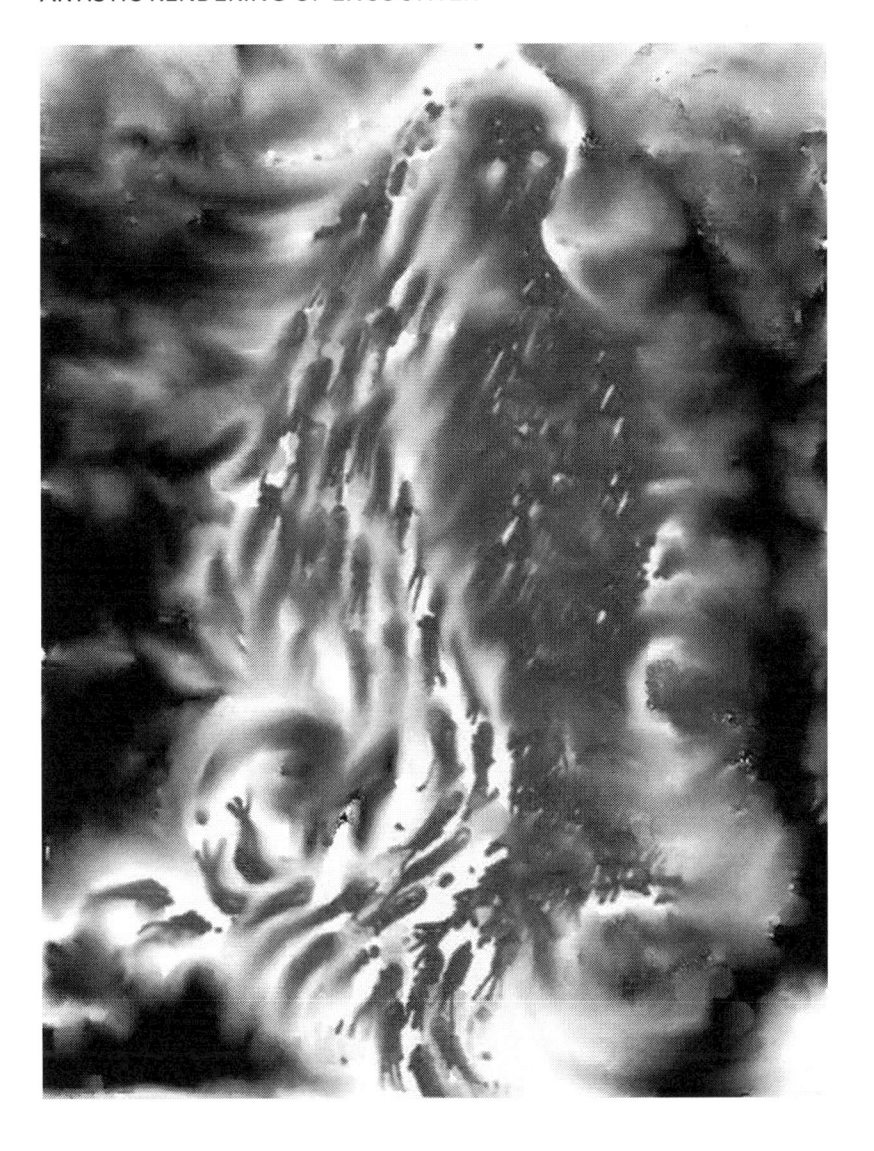

ARTISTIC RENDERING OF ENCOUNTER

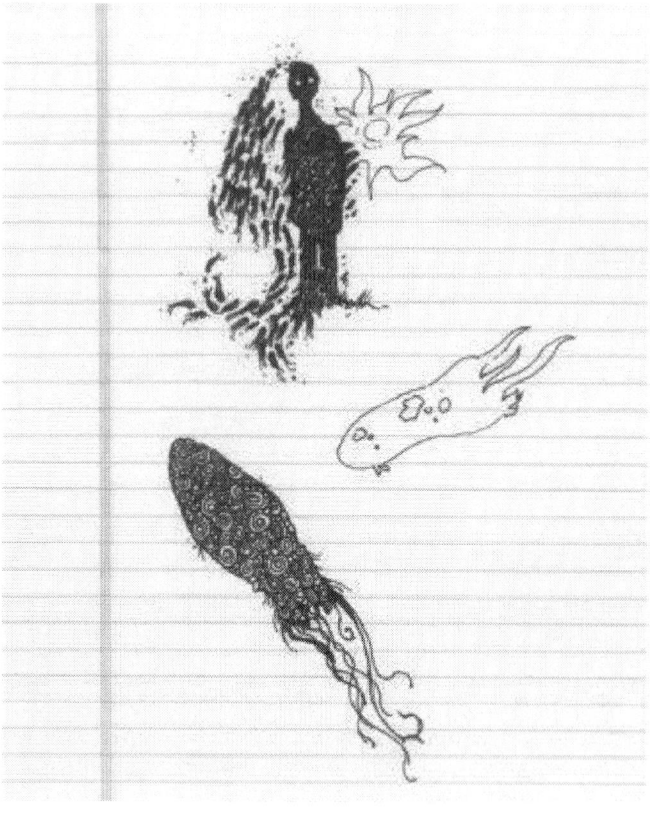

The drawings above were made by the same individual who provided the previous sketch. After he allowed himself to be subjected to hypnosis, he was able to produce a more detailed depiction of the entity which accosted both him and his companions. In each of these sketches, he attempts to capture the image of both the entity and the squid-like organism which he believes to have been implanted into this brain. According to his recollection, while this entity took over control of his mind and body, it inserted a squid-like creature up and into his nose, which then penetrated his brain. When I asked this individual if he had any intention of having this creature removed, he was adamant to the contrary, stating he feels a symbiotic relationship to it and continues to gain enlightenment from its presence.

In the first drawing, Papa Croc attempts to recreate the image of the entity not as a solid mass, but as a joining of hundred or perhaps thousands of these squid-like creatures. My brother describes a similar entity which appeared outside our tent, the details of which are provided in the Encounters section of this book. The second drawing shows both the large entity and then two different renderings of the smaller entities. The third drawing, though overall consisting of less detail and a more general image of both entities, includes a depiction of the process by which the larger entity took control of the individual's body and the means by which the smaller entity was inserted.

The sketch above was provided by a Ranch security guard with whom I had established a working relationship. According to him, he was performing his nightly rounds when he suddenly felt a strong sense of dread, as if he was in the presence of something foreboding. While he did not actually see this entity, he sensed it as large, black, and indistinct with regard to features and details. Regardless, notice its resemblance to the figures drawn by Papa Croc, including the elongated fingers and the all black body.

DOG-MAN

This sketch is an eye-witness depiction of the Bray Road beast, a dog-man creature that has been observed by residents of Wisconsin. From what I have gleaned from the descriptions of the locals in and around Fort Duchesne, the Skinwalker, while moving upright, might appear similar.

One interesting story I was told claims a man driving late at night near the Ranch supposedly encountered two such beasts standing next to each other and apparently talking. As he slowed his truck to get a better look, he was dumbstruck to see that one of them was smoking a cigarette.

PETROGRAPHS AND PETRO-GLYPHS

These are just two samples of the many rock drawings which can be found all throughout the Uintah Basin, and the Four Corners, in general. In the first are depicted three different forms of the Skinwalker. Notice that all three have horns, indicating the bison as the primary totem. All three of the figures are also shown with swirling lines or concentric circles originating from their right hands. While there are those who believe these circles are merely crude representations of shields—note what looks to be a spear in the left hand of the largest of the figures, there are others who believe these circles are actually portals being opened. In support of the later, while Skinwalkers were thought to be spies, often sneaking up on the settlements of their enemies, there is little reference to them fulfilling roles as warriors or hunters, which would minimize their need for spears and shields.

The second drawing clearly shows a figure which resembles the common depiction of aliens as they often appear today. Notice the distinct shape of the head and the eyes. Keep in mind, too, that these petroglyphs and petro-graphs are literally thousands of years old, which lends credence to the belief that aliens may have visited the Earth long before man became aware of the heavens, and that their association with the Four Corners, and specifically the area of Utah in which the Ranch is located, may not be a coincidence.

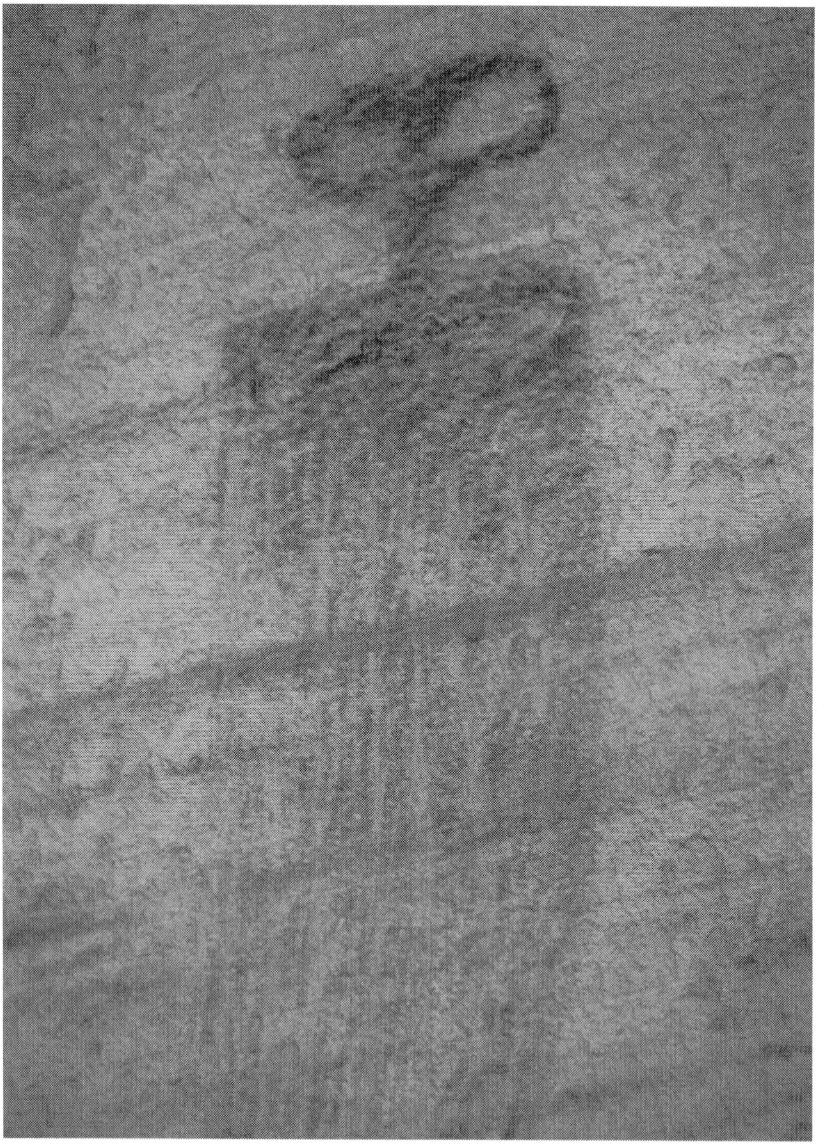

FORMATIONS AND PHENOMENA

STONE FORMATIONS

It is my opinion that both of these structures are manmade and served a particular purpose at one time. The first photo may have been a shelter of some sort, or even the remains of a much larger structure of spiritual significance. The second photo, I believe, is the remains of an ancient road leading along the path of the Skinwalker. I walked the length of this road multiple times hoping to increase my chances at encountering the phenomena. Both structures have since suffered the ravages of time.

ANCIENT ROAD

This photo reveals the extent of the ancient road shown in the previous photo. Not only does it lie on the path of the Skinwalker, as professed by the Native Americans indigenous to the area, but one actually leads directly to Werewolf Ridge and the other to the Old Homestead. The Natives consider these roads taboo and do not go there. I have had many opportunities to walk this path, and always experience a deep sense of mystery and foreboding. There is also historic reference to roads traveled by the Anazasi, all of which led north and seemed to end without a specific destination, leading to the belief that these were actually the roads traveled by the dead as they crossed over into the afterlife.

ICE CIRCLE

Ice circle found in the water canal next to the Skinwalker ranch homestead. The NIDS' investigators while walking the property found this perfectly etched circle in the frozen waters of the canal. The Shermans allegedly found similar circles on the Ranch property itself. There is some suggestion they may have UFO implications. Regardless, their geometric precision is rare and unusual.

MUTILATED CALF

Mutilated calves and cows are a common occurrence throughout the Four Corners area. This photo illustrates the extent of these mutilations. Notice, also, that the left ear of this calf has been severed. While some official investigators point to this particular trauma as evidence of poaching— ranchers tend to tag the left ear of their stock, other wounds and incisions, for example the extraction of the eye, removal of the anus, and uterus, tend to suggest otherwise. The informant with whom I have had multiple conversations is under the impression that these mutilations are perpetrated by aliens, and that our government and military are not only aware of their involvement but permit and encourage it. However, the narrative provided by Jane relating the fate of her dogs and horses suggests otherwise.

I, as do others, believe that these mutilations are attributable to a hostile intelligence. In the case of this particular calf, it was seen in proximity to its mother by an investigator only a half-hour before it was slaughtered. According to that investigator, he left the area to perform other duties and when he returned he found the calf as shown in the photo. Despite the extent of the mutilation, no blood was found on the ground. An autopsy revealed the mutilation was accomplished using an extremely sharp surgical knife and an unidentified and blunt tool. Attempts to replicate the scene by pouring blood onto the same ground and measuring the time it took to absorb and dry failed to reproduce any of the variables of the actual mutilation. Due to these variables and the circumstances described by the investigator, human involvement was ruled out.

ABOUT THE AUTHOR

RYAN SKINNER began his research into the phenomena at Skinwalker Ranch in 2008. Since the events chronicled in this book, he has returned numerous times each year to Utah's Uintah Basin to conduct field investigations. While there he spends several weeks in his specially equipped RV, camping alone in the desert, trying to find answers to whatever lurks in Fort Duchesne's nearby mesas and valleys. In September of 2009, Ryan created the web domain names www.skinwalkerranch.org and www.skinwalkerranch.com; paranormal websites which promote discussions on Skinwalker Ranch related topics. The website challenges visitors to think outside of the modern-day paradigm regarding the possibility of alien life as it relates to human consciousness and multiple dimensions. On April of 2011, Ryan received his Private Pilot's License and uses it to survey other unexplored hotspots throughout the United States. In 1999, he graduated from Eastern New Mexico University with a Bachelor's Degree of Science and received a Major in Public Speaking and a Minor in Theatre. He graduated with Honors, earning the title Magna Cum Laude. This is Mr. Skinner's second book. He anticipates writing additional true stories chronicling not only his own past, present, and future adventures but those of others who have experienced the paranormal. Mr. Skinner does NOT condone trespassing on or around the Ranch.

Ryan Skinner has been featured on several nationally recognized television programs. In 2012 he was featured as a "Skinwalker Ranch Expert" on the *Jesse Ventura's Conspiracy Theory* which aired December 3rd on TrueTv. In 2013 he helped produce and was also the featured "Skinwalker Guide" for the *Joe Rogan Questions Everything* show which was televised August 21st, on the SyFy Channel. He has also headlined various radio shows, and podcasts. As a producer, entertainer, and now author; Ryan Skinner hopes to continue his search for answers for many years to come, and invites you to watch him on his paranormal journeys. Ryan currently resides in Milton Wisconsin, where he lives with his two children, Whitney and Max.

You can view more pictures, stories and videos of his adventures and learn more about Skinwalker Ranch and the lore of the Skinwalker by visiting his website at: http://www.skinwalkerranch.com

Thank You for reading Ryan Skinner's third book related to the topic of Skinwalker Ranch and his research on the lore and phenomena associated with the location and that of the Four Corners. If you enjoyed reading this book, your positive review (click here) would be appreciated.

Ryan Skinner

Printed in Poland
by Amazon Fulfillment
Poland Sp. z o.o., Wrocław
03 November 2022

0adc05d3-d8cb-4c04-ac8b-a3b8acf11672R01